Lecture Notes in Economics and Mathematical Systems

For information about Vols. 1–128, please contact your bookseller or Springer-Verlag

Vol. 129: H.-J. Lüthi, Komplementaritäts- und Fixpunktalgorithmen in der mathematischen Programmierung. Spieltheorie und Ökonomie. VII, 145 Seiten. 1976.

Vol. 130: Multiple Criteria Decision Making, Jouy-en-Josas, France. Proceedings 1975. Edited by H. Thiriez and S. Zionts. VI, 409 pages. 1976.

Vol. 131: Mathematical Systems Theory. Proceedings 1975. Edited by G. Marchesini and S. K. Mitter. X, 408 pages. 1976.

Vol. 132: U. H. Funke, Mathematical Models in Marketing. A Collection of Abstracts. XX, 514 pages. 1976.

Vol. 133: Warsaw Fall Seminars in Mathematical Economics 1975. Edited by M. W. Los, J. Los, and A. Wieczorek. V. 159 pages. 1976.

Vol. 134: Computing Methods in Applied Sciences and Engineering. Proceedings 1975. VIII, 390 pages. 1976.

Vol. 135: H. Haga, A Disequilibrium – Equilibrium Model with Money and Bonds. A Keynesian – Walrasian Synthesis. VI, 119 pages. 1976.

Vol. 136: E. Kofler und G. Menges, Entscheidungen bei unvollständiger Information. XII, 357 Seiten. 1976.

Vol. 137: R. Wets, Grundlagen Konvexer Optimierung. VI, 146 Seiten. 1976.

Vol. 138: K. Okuguchi, Expectations and Stability in Oligopoly Models. VI, 103 pages. 1976.

Vol. 139: Production Theory and Its Applications. Proceedings. Edited by H. Albach and G. Bergendahl. VIII, 193 pages. 1977.

Vol. 140: W. Eichhorn and J. Voeller, Theory of the Price Index. Fisher's Test Approach and Generalizations. VII, 95 pages. 1976.

Vol. 141: Mathematical Economics and Game Theory. Essays in Honor of Oskar Morgenstern. Edited by R. Henn and O. Moeschlin. XIV, 703 pages. 1977.

Vol. 142: J. S. Lane, On Optimal Population Paths. V, 123 pages. 1977.

Vol. 143: B. Näslund, An Analysis of Economic Size Distributions. XV, 100 pages. 1977.

Vol. 144: Convex Analysis and Its Applications. Proceedings 1976. Edited by A. Auslender. VI, 219 pages. 1977.

Vol. 145: J. Rosenmüller, Extreme Games and Their Solutions. IV, 126 pages. 1977.

Vol. 146: In Search of Economic Indicators. Edited by W. H. Strigel. XVI, 198 pages. 1977.

Vol. 147: Resource Allocation and Division of Space. Proceedings. Edited by T. Fujii and R. Sato. VIII, 184 pages. 1977.

Vol. 148: C. E. Mandl, Simulationstechnik und Simulationsmodelle in den Sozial- und Wirtschaftswissenschaften. IX, 173 Seiten. 1977.

Vol. 149: Stationäre und schrumpfende Bevölkerungen: Demographisches Null- und Negativwachstum in Österreich. Herausgegeben von G. Feichtinger. VI, 262 Seiten. 1977.

Vol. 150: Bauer et al., Supercritical Wing Sections III. VI, 179 pages. 1977.

Vol. 151: C. A. Schneeweiß, Inventory-Production Theory. VI, 116 pages. 1977.

Vol. 152: Kirsch et al., Notwendige Optimalitätsbedingungen und ihre Anwendung. VI, 157 Seiten. 1978.

Vol. 153: Kombinatorische Entscheidungsprobleme: Methoden und Anwendungen. Herausgegeben von T. M. Liebling und M. Rössler. VIII, 206 Seiten. 1978.

Vol. 154: Problems and Instruments of Business Cycle Analysis. Proceedings 1977. Edited by W. H. Strigel. VI, 442 pages. 1978.

Vol. 155: Multiple Criteria Problem Solving. Proceedings 1977. Edited by S. Zionts. VIII, 567 pages. 1978.

Vol. 156: B. Näslund and B. Sellstedt, Neo-Ricardian Theory. With Applications to Some Current Economic Problems. VI, 165 pages. 1978.

Vol. 157: Optimization and Operations Research. Proceedings 1977. Edited by R. Henn, B. Korte, and W. Oettli. VI, 270 pages. 1978.

Vol. 158: L. J. Cherene, Set Valued Dynamical Systems and Economic Flow. VIII, 83 pages. 1978.

Vol. 159: Some Aspects of the Foundations of General Equilibrium Theory: The Posthumous Papers of Peter J. Kalman. Edited by J. Green. VI, 167 pages. 1978.

Vol. 160: Integer Programming and Related Areas. A Classified Bibliography. Edited by D. Hausmann. XIV, 314 pages. 1978.

Vol. 161: M. J. Beckmann, Rank in Organizations. VIII, 164 pages. 1978.

Vol. 162: Recent Developments in Variable Structure Systems, Economics and Biology. Proceedings 1977. Edited by R. R. Mohler and A. Ruberti. VI, 326 pages. 1978.

Vol. 163: G. Fandel, Optimale Entscheidungen in Organisationen. VI, 143 Seiten. 1979.

Vol. 164: C. L. Hwang and A. S. M. Masud, Multiple Objective Decision Making – Methods and Applications. A State-of-the-Art Survey. XII, 351 pages. 1979.

Vol. 165: A. Maravall, Identification in Dynamic Shock-Error Models. VIII, 158 pages. 1979.

Vol. 166: R. Cuninghame-Green, Minimax Algebra. XI, 258 pages. 1979.

Vol. 167: M. Faber, Introduction to Modern Austrian Capital Theory. X, 196 pages. 1979.

Vol. 168: Convex Analysis and Mathematical Economics. Proceedings 1978. Edited by J. Kriens. V, 136 pages. 1979.

Vol. 169: A. Rapoport et al., Coalition Formation by Sophisticated Players. VII, 170 pages. 1979.

Vol. 170: A. E. Roth, Axiomatic Models of Bargaining. V, 121 pages. 1979.

Vol. 171: G. F. Newell, Approximate Behavior of Tandem Queues. XI, 410 pages. 1979.

Vol. 172: K. Neumann and U. Steinhardt, GERT Networks and the Time-Oriented Evaluation of Projects. 268 pages. 1979.

Vol. 173: S. Erlander, Optimal Spatial Interaction and the Gravity Model. VII, 107 pages. 1980.

Vol. 174: Extremal Methods and Systems Analysis. Edited by A. V. Fiacco and K. O. Kortanek. XI, 545 pages. 1980.

Vol. 175: S. K. Srinivasan and R. Subramanian, Probabilistic Analysis of Redundant Systems. VII, 356 pages. 1980.

Vol. 176: R. Färe, Laws of Diminishing Returns. VIII, 97 pages. 1980.

Vol. 177: Multiple Criteria Decision Making-Theory and Application. Proceedings, 1979. Edited by G. Fandel and T. Gal. XVI, 570 pages. 1980.

Vol. 178: M. N. Bhattacharyya, Comparison of Box-Jenkins and Bonn Monetary Model Prediction Performance. VII, 146 pages. 1980.

Vol. 179: Recent Results in Stochastic Programming. Proceedings, 1979. Edited by P. Kall and A. Prékopa. IX, 237 pages. 1980.

Vol. 180: J. F. Brotchie, J. W. Dickey and R. Sharpe, TOPAZ – General Planning Technique and its Applications at the Regional, Urban, and Facility Planning Levels. VII, 356 pages. 1980.

Vol. 181: H. D. Sherali and C. M. Shetty, Optimization with Disjunctive Constraints. VIII, 156 pages. 1980.

Vol. 182: J. Wolters, Stochastic Dynamic Properties of Linear Econometric Models. VIII, 154 pages. 1980.

Vol. 183: K. Schittkowski, Nonlinear Programming Codes. VIII, 242 pages. 1980.

continuation on page 107

Lecture Notes
in Economics and
Mathematical Systems

Managing Editors: M. Beckmann and W. Krelle

268

Volker Firchau

Information Evaluation in Capital Markets

Author

Dr. Volker Firchau
Universität Augsburg
Memminger Str. 14, D-8900 Augsburg, FRG

ISBN 978-3-540-16462-3 ISBN 978-3-642-49272-3 (eBook)
DOI 10.1007/978-3-642-49272-3

2142/3140-543210

Preface

An investor who wants to invest a certain amount and to whom a lot of more or less risky alternatives arise would divide this amount among several securities. He makes this portfolio decision because of his expectations with regard to these assets which result from the information available to him. If the investor obtains additional information, then his knowledge would improve and, therefore, the portfolio decision made by him. Accordingly, he will be ready to accept certain costs related to the information procurement. The value of information indicates the maximum tolerable information costs, and its knowledge, therefore, enables - by comparing with the actual information costs - to evaluate the profitability of an information procurement.

In this book, the value of information for the problem of portfolio planning is explicitly determined, namely as well for the case of fixed prices not influenced by the information activity as within the scope of a market model. These explicit results allow several conclusions, in particular about the influence of preknowledge, risk aversion, information precision and information dissemination on their value.

The Bayesian decision theory is the basis for this paper. Correspondingly, a subjective concept of probability is underlying, and the information processing and evaluation is understood in a statistical sense. As one might expect, the question about the correctness of an information is not treated, although manipulating the asset prices by deliberate disinformation can be observed in practice and is, certainly, an interesting problem.

The so-called hybrid model of the capital market which is taken as a basis is founded on the two assumptions of constant absolute risk aversion and of normally distributed rates of return. These very strong assumptions are required for the deduction of the explicit results. The conclusions deduced from this, in particular, the ones of qualitative type, should, however, remain valid approximately also if these assumptions are violated.

I would like to give my sincere thanks to Professor Dr. G. Bamberg for encouraging me to occupy myself with the problem of the capital market theory and for many precious hints. I thank Mrs. B. Emmrich for the careful typing and the Springer Verlag for the friendly support.

Augsburg, December 1985 Volker Firchau

TABLE OF CONTENTS

Used Symbols

u	utility function, here always exponential
α	constant, absolute risk aversion
v	prices at the beginning of the period
X	stochastic prices at the end of the period
w	initial wealth
r	riskless interest rate
y	portfolio vector
g	result function, here always end-of-period wealth
φ	prior density of the end-of-period prices, here always normal
φ_z	posterior density of the end-of-period prices
μ	prior expectation vector of the end-of-period prices
Ω	prior covariance matrix of the end-of-period prices
Φ	set of possible prior densities
ν	certainty equivalent
m	prior expectation vector of μ
Π	prior covariance matrix of μ
L	opportunity costs
Z	information system
z	information
f_x	likelihood density of Z
f	marginal density of Z
Σ	covariance matrix of the information system
T	transformation matrix
$H(\varphi,Z)$	amount of information
M	group of all investors
N	group of all informed investors
d_N	fraction of all informed investors (measured by the risk aversion)
A^T	transpose of the matrix A
$\|A\|$	determinant of the matrix A

1. Introduction and Summary

1.1 Portfolio Planning and Capital Market Models as Problems of Decision Theory

Single-period portfolio planning means the unique determination of the single amounts which are to be invested into different offered assets. The objective is an as high as possible wealth increase, or - equivalently to this - a maximum rate of return with regard to the invested capital. Portfolio planning, therefore, shows as a typical decision problem.

The description of the based decision space, i.e. the set of possible decisions, is no problem. If necessary, conditions have to be considered which limit the single amounts or the total amount to be invested. From the decision theoretic point of view it is more interesting that the specification of the result which is relevant for the evaluation of a decision, i.e. the end-of-period wealth, is immediately possible. This one is a linear function as well of the decision variables as of the rates of return or - for given initial prices - of the end-of-period prices of the assets. Therefore, it has an analytically very simple form.

If the end-of-period prices are known, a deterministic decision problem results. Then, it shows to be optimal, to invest only into the asset with the highest return where for an unlimited decision space no optimal solution exists,[1] if refinancing any amount at a lower interest rate is possible. If such 'free lunches'[2] are realistically excluded, then from this the equality of the rates of return of all assets results, at least if short sales are admitted.[3] Then, obviously, no real decision problem appears. The consequences of all decisions are equal, and, therefore, all decisions are equally good. The treatment of the portfolio planning problem as a deterministic decision problem, however, is not only theoretically not interesting, but also practically meaningless,

---

1) See for example Jakob, Smith [1972], Bawa, Goroff [1983].

2) For the meaning of no-arbitrage concepts as basis of capital market theory see Wilhelm [1981,1983].

3) Also if short sales are excluded, the equality of all equilibrium returns can be shown in the scope of a suitable market model, see for example Rudolph [1983].

because the true prices realizing at the end of the period, are nearly alwa s unknown at the point of decision, e.g. at the beginning of the period.

Therefore, in the following, *portfolioplanning* is understood as a decision problem under uncertainty, and first of all as a *decision problem under risk*. Consequently, it is started from the principle that the decider indeed does not surely know the true end-of-period prices, but that he presents his preknowledge in the form of a subjective prior distribution which describes the probabilities for the possible realizations of the prices from his point of view.

If one assumes risk neutrality, i.e. if one presumes that the investor evaluates the assets only by their expected returns, then the same unrealistic results yield as if one completely knows the true returns. Again, it would be invested only into one asset, indeed into the one with the highest expected return. A real portfolio, as it appears intuitively meaningful for reasons of the risk sharing and as it is also generally observed in practice, would not at all result.

A realistic description of investment behavior has, therefore, also to consider the risks related to an investment decision, in fact in the sense that a *riskaverse attitude* of the investor is assumed.

Markowitz [1952], therefore, proposed in his paper which is pioneering for the development of modern capital market theory to consider the return variance as relevant risk measure.[1] This leads to the consideration of decision rules which evaluate a stochastic result only with the aid of its expectated value and its variance, and which are summarized under the term (μ,σ)-principle. Such (μ,σ)-rules which are called 'classic' in the decision theory have the advantage to require no assumptions about the underlying distribution,[2] but the disadvantage not to satisfy the dominance principle.[3]

---

1) Rothschild, Stiglitz [1970] consider other possiblities to describe the phenomenon risk.

2) except the existence of expectation and variance. This assumption is not quite uncritical. So, the consideration of the class of the stable distributions, whose elements do not have a finite variance except for the normal distribution is useful in portfolio theory, see Fama [1965], Jensen [1969], Ross [1978], Dybvig, Ingersoll jr. [1982], Bawa, Goroff [1983], Chamberlain [1983].

3) if any distributions are admitted, see Philippatos, Gressis [1974], Colson, Zeleny [1980] and Bawa [1982] who presents a comprehensive survey about the literature published about 'Stochastic Dominance' problems.

In spite of these theoretic deficiencies the principle of Markowitz's approach, namely understanding the portfolio problem as a decision problem under risk, showed to be extremely fruitful. Subsequently, Sharpe [1964], Lintner [1965], and Mossin [1966] developed the *Capital Asset Pricing Model* (CAPM) which represents the core of the modern capital market theory. Elton, Gruber [1979] give a good survey about the variety of the problems and the areas of research initiated by Markowitz's paper. A big number of monographs and textbooks[1] make evident the acceptance reached in the meantime and the significance of the portfolio theory and the capital market theory based on it, but also the fact that books which are actually planned as a general presentation of decision theory dedicate more and more own paragraphs to this topic.[2]

The conception of portfolio planning as a decision problem under risk suggests not to limit oneself to classic decision principles but to try to describe the risk attitude of the investor by a Bernoulli utility function and to evaluate the portfolio decisions with the aid of the expected utility of the end-of-period wealth. If one demands the compatibility with the (μ,σ)-principle,[3] and if one admits any distribution for the end-of-period prices, then, according to a well known result of Schneeweiß [1967] only a quadratic utility function is possible.[4] This one badly fails in not being monotonously increasing.[5] If one wants to keep the compatibility with the (μ,σ)-principle and to avoid the problems related to the quadratic utility function, then there remains as an alternative only to confine the class of admitted distributions.[6]

---

1) for example Sharpe [1970], Mossin [1973], Saelzle [1976], Rudolph [1979], Drukarczyk [1980], Swoboda [1981], Wilhelm [1983].

2) for example Pratt, Raiffa, Schlaifer [1965], Sinn [1980], Bitz [1981], Laux [1982].

3) i.e. the expected utility is a function only of the expectation and of the variance of the end-of-period wealth.

4) see also Saelzle [1976]. Approximately, also other utility functions can be compatible with (μ,σ)-rules. In practice, these approximations can be completely sufficient, see for example Levy, Markowitz [1979], Pulley [1983].

5) Because of the above mentioned violation of the dominance principle, obviously, no monotonously increasing utility function which is compatible with the (μ,σ)-principle for any distribution can exist.

6) see Dybvig, Ingersoll jr. [1982].

In the following, it is always assumed that the *end-of-period prices* are *normally distributed* and that the associated covariance matrix is positive definite. Therefore, no perfect correlations exist between the prices. As mentioned above, here, a subjective prior distribution is imputed for the considered investor. Empirical investigations of share price developments which suggest another type of distribution,[1] do not disprove this assumption. Even if a sufficiently precise estimation of the objective price distributions is possible[2] and is available to the investor, then his expectations generally represent a compromise between the objective data and his personal (pre)conceptions.[3] The reasons for the assumption of normal distribution which is also mostly presumed in the literature are on the one hand the *stability* under linear transformation, i.e. the end-of-period wealth of any portfolio is always normally distributed.[4] On the other hand, the normal distributions form a so-called (μ,σ)-class,[5] i.e. each utility function leads to a (μ,σ)-rule, if one confines to the class of normal distributions.

In addition to the assumption of normal distribution, in the following, an *exponential utility function* [6] is assumed for all considered investors. These two assumptions characterize the *hybrid model* so denoted by Bamberg and Spremann [1981]. The following items are decisive for taking the hybrid model approach as a basis:

---

1) see for example Jensen [1969], Perry [1983].

2) regarding estimation problems, especially under stationarity aspects, see Jobson, Korkie [1980], Levy, Kroll [1980], Hsu [1982], Maier, Peterson, Van der Weide [1982], Cohen, Hawawini, Maier, Schwartz, Whitcomb [1983].

3) An attempt to model this behavior is found at Owen, Rabinovitch [1980]. The paper of Peterson, Peterson [1982] contains approaches to an empirical investigation of the subjective expectations of the investors.

4) Generally, the elliptic distributions fulfill this stability requirement, see Owen, Rabinovitch [1983]. The disagreable property that any real numbers are admitted as realizations of the stochastic prices, cannot be avoided. Thus, for example, the truncated normal distributions are no more stable in this sense, see Norgaad, Killeen [1980].

5) each one-dimensional normal distribution is uniquely characterized by its expectation and variance, see Schweeweiß [1967].

6) i.e. each investor has a constant absolute risk aversion, see Pratt [1964], Arrow [1965].

- The exponential utility function, besides the linear utility function which is not suitable here, is the only one which fulfills the *consistence axiom*,[1] which secures the independency of the optimal portfolio decision from the initial wealth.[2]
- The exponential utility function always allows like the linear utility function an *explicit determination of the expected value of information* which exactly in this case is independent of the initial wealth of the investor.[3]
- The exponential utility function secures the validity of the *separation theorem*.[4] More precisely, the following is true: In a single-period model, the separation theorem holds, if any distributions are admitted, if and only if the utility function comes from the HARA[5]-class (Cass, Stiglitz [1970]).
- The hybrid model allows the *explicit determination of the optimal portfolio decision*. Epps [1981] showed this property (in a sense to be precised) together with the compatiblity with the (μ,σ)-principle uniquely characterizes the hybrid model.[6]
- If the prices at the beginning of the period are not presupposed exogenously, but are conceived as equilibrium prices within the scope of a capital market model, then the hybrid model approach also allows the *explicit determination of these equilibrium prices*. Only by this, an explicit determination of the expected value of information will be possible for the case that the information activity influences the equilibrium prices about the changes of the individual expectations.

---

1) see Pfanzagl [1959], a reduction comes from Bamberg, Spremann [1981], see also Spremann, Bamberg [1983b].

2) This property, of course, also evokes criticism, see Bitz [1981].

3) See LaValle [1968], Hilton [1981], Bamberg, Spremann [1983]. But also for other utility functions - at least in special cases - an explicit determination of the expected value of information is possible, see for example Morris [1974].

4) see Tobin [1958], Merton [1972], Buchner [1982], Franke [1983]. The separation theorem can also be concluded only from the assumption of normal distribution, see Ross [1978].

5) Hyperbolic absolute risk aversion, the constant absolute risk aversion is a special case of it.

6) A simplification of the assumptions and a modification of the proof is due to Bamberg [1983].

- Also if the prior information is not precised in form of a unique normal distribution, but by a set of possible normal distributions,[1] the optimal portfolio and the expected value of information can explicitly be determined[2] within the scope of a hybrid model thus modified.

In addition to the assumptions of the hybrid model a *perfect capital market* which is characterized by the following premises (see for example Franke [1983]) is taken as a basis:

- No transaction costs and taxes occur.
- The investors are price-takers: The prices at the beginning of the period - whether presumed exogenously or defined as equilibrium prices - are not directly influenced by the individual portfolio decisions.
- Assets can be bought or sold in any quantity or fraction.
- The market prices are the same for all investors.
- There exists a riskless interest rate at which investors can lend or borrow any amounts.

The determination of optimal portfolios or the analysis of capital market models is also possible if some of these assumptions are weakened. The following, in no way complete selection of contributions to the theory of non-perfect capital markets proves this. Thus, for example Brennan [1975], Cooper, Farhangian [1982], Patel, Subrahwanyam [1982], Blog, van der Hoek, Rinnooy Kan [1983] treat the problem of portfolioplanning if transaction costs are to be considered.[3] It shows that, by this, the number of shares which make up the portfolio is strongly limited. Rudolph [1982] and Spremann, Bamberg [1983a] investigate the influence of monopolistic

---

1) For the foundation of this approach of partial information and the decision principle related to it, see Bierlein [1963], Richter [1963], Kofler, Menges [1976], Kofler, Menges, Fahrion, Huschens, Kuß [1980].

2) regarding possibilities of determining the optimal portfolio within the scope of the classic (μ,σ)-approach, see Bühler [1977,1984].

3) Schnabel [1981] investigates the influence of transaction costs on the equilibrium prices.

competition on the price development. Brennan [1971] and - within the scope of the hybrid model - Bamberg, Firchau [1981] treat the case of different borrowing and lending rates. Considering taxes and stochastic bankruptcy costs Kim [1978] shows the relevance of the capital structure[1] for the firm value, see also Spremann, Bamberg [1980].

From the assumptions generally made there is actually only one missing namely the one of information efficiency. This one says that the entire relevant information is available free-of-charge for each investor and already reflected fully in the prices at each moment.[2] All investors have as rationally acting individuals at all instants correspondingly equal expectations. This requirement of *information efficiency* is *not* demanded here. The main topic of this book, in opposition to this, is: How is information to be evaluated which is not necessarily available to all investors? The theoretical reason of assuming the information efficiency hypothesis is that only in this way homogeneous expectations for all investors can be proved. This property considerably simplifies the theoretical as the empirical treatment of the problems, but contradicts to the entire practical experience.[3] Correspondingly, in the following, always *inhomogeneous expectations* of the investors are assumed where the homogeneity is included as (unlikely) special case. Discarding the homogeneity assumption, in more general capital market models, the analysis of otherwise relatively unproblematic questions can be made considerably more difficult.[4] As Lintner [1969] showed, admitting inhomogeneous expectations, however, is within the scope of the hybrid model possible without difficulties.

One aspect of the information efficiency, however, is maintained, in the following. If the expectations of a group of investors are

---

1) not present if assuming a perfect capital market, see Modigliani, Miller [1958].

2) see Fama [1970]. Some authors count - differently from here - the information efficiency to the premises characterizing a perfect capital market, see for example Drukarcyk [1980].

3) see Tobin [1983].

4) see for example Gonedes [1976], Swoboda [1982].

changed because of additional information, then this leads to a change of the equilibrium prices, indeed immediately. After information increase there can only be bought and sold according to the new equilibrium prices. Correspondingly, the prices, in fact, do not completely reflect the entire information, but at each instant the information status of the whole market.

Summarizing it results that, in the following, a perfect capital market is always assumed, and that all investors have exponential utility functions and normally distributed, generally individually different expectations.

1.2 Information and Information Evaluation

Information, also called *news*, is the result of an information process. This result is characteristically ex ante unknown. Within the framework of a statistical theory such processes are described by random variables. The information process, also designated by *information system*, is a random variable and the information in fact obtained is the realization of this random variable. One can only speak about an information system that supplies information about the considered decision problem, if the statistical relation between the news and the unknown state - here the end-of-period prices - is known. Correspondingly, an information system is completely described only by specifying the distributions of the news dependent on the states.[1] The Bayes formula then outlines the transition from the prior distribution (before receiving the information) to a posterior distribution (after receiving information). The comparison between the prior and posterior distribution illustrates the influence of the information on the expectations of the decider. If an information process takes place, then it is chronologically before decision making. After having received the information, the decision is made because of the posterior distribution, therefore considering the information. Correspondingly, within the framework of a decision theoretic model, only the pragmatic content[2] of an information is interesting. Information is serviceable knowledge.[3]

---

[1] i.e. by specifying the likelihood function.

[2] opposite to the semantic content which is based upon in the information theory founded by Shannon [1948], see also Wild [1971].

[3] see Wittmann [1959].

An information system is meaningless without a decision problem to be solved and to which the information is related.

Information systems and information are, therefore, conceived in an analytical-statistical, pragmatic sense. Only descriptive working up and aggregation of known data is not dealt with here although such information is in practice not unsignificant, contributes surely to clearness and, hence, really improves the decision basis.

Within the framework of the assumed capital market model, in the following, first of all, unbiased normally distributed estimators of the end-of-period prices or of linear aggregations of these prices are considered as information systems. By this, the estimation of all or of single prices is also included as the forecast of index developments. In the same way information can be treated which first of all does not represent a price forecast, but enables such a forecast.[1] In order not to leave the hybrid model, it is necessary to admit only such information systems which lead from normally distributed prior distributions to normally distributed posterior distributions in any case. The above mentioned relatively big class of information systems fulfills this. A satisfactory approximation of real information systems should be possible by this. Also if - as above addressed - the prior information is not given in form of a single distribution, but in the sense of Kofler, Menges [1976] in form of a partial information, the influence of information of the above addressed manner on the portfolio decision can be described and evaluated.

The *expected value of information* (EVI) specifies the maximal tolerable information cost, i.e. the amount is determined at which the investor is indifferent between making the decision without information and with information connected with the payment of this amount. The EVI is to be determined ex ante in order to enable a decision making by comparing with the actual information cost. Hence, it has to be compared the optimal value of the objective function (here the expected

---

1) Examples for such information are - with respect to an asset - annual reports and financial statements, but also - market related - market forecasts, orders of certain industry branches and the like. Direct price forecasts are partly attempted by the 'classic' stock market information services, the economic magazines, but also by the mordern computer-aided information systems.

utility of the end-of-period wealth) before information access with the *expected* optimal value of the objective function after information access. This definition of the EVI is due to Marschak [1954] who also firstly showed that the EVI is always non-negative, if the data of the decision problem is not changed by the information activity.[1] If within the scope of a capital market model the equilibrium prices and, therefore, the result function change, negative information values can occur, as will be shown. The same is true if a decision space changed by the information process is assumed, as Blau [1974] shows for a general stochastic optimization problem. After a controversial discussion in the literature,[2] which can be considered as finished by Bitz [1975], this definition of the EVI is generally accepted today.

Whilst it can be started from a linear utility function the determination of the EVI is usually not a problem - in any case not more difficult than solving the underlying decision problem. Also with only partial knowledge of the decision data the EVI can still be estimated (Firchau [1980b]). For the case of an arbitrary non-linear utility function the definition, however, only supplies an implicit equation for the EVI. Not even the existence or uniqueness of a solution is cecured in any case. If an exponential utility function is given, then the explicit determination of the EVI, however, is always possible (see above).

Within the framework of the information theory the *amount of information* which specifies the entropy reduction is used as relevant information measure. The amount of information is the bigger the 'more surprising' the message is on average. As a purely semantic information measure the amount of information is independent of the underlying decision problem. Hence, this one is usually not suitable as a basis for evaluating the profitability of the information process.[3] However, there are some relations between the expected value of information and the amount of information. On the one hand, relatively general monotony relations which can be normally described by inequalities can be concluded.[4] On the other hand, under special

---

1) see Albach [1961], Niggemann [1973] and - for more general uncertainty functions and optimality criteria - DeGroot [1962], Firchau [1980a].

2) see for example Albach [1969], Rehberg [1973], Teichmann [1973].

3) see Lindley [1955], Marschak [1959,1971], Ackoff [1968], Mag [1977].

4) see Grettenberg [1962], Behara [1974], Firchau [1980a].

assumptions about the form of the utility function, the proportionality of both information measures can be shown. For the logarithmic utility function, this is examined in the papers of Kelly [1956], Arrow [1972], Smith [1974], Bernardo [1979], and Wahl [1983]. Also for the completely different, here presumed hybrid model approach such a proportionality can be shown for the case of exogeneously given, by the information process uninfluenced prices at the beginning of the period.[1)]

Also for more general optimality criteria, pragmatic information values similar to the EVI can be defined, for example for the above addressed case of only partial information about the prior distribution.[2)]

In this book, the expected value of information is examined for two basic situations. Firstly, it is assumed within the framework of the portfolio approach that the exogeneously given prices at the beginning of the period are not influenced by the information process. This assumption can be justified if only a single investor or a small group of investors are informed whose risk aversion compared with the one of the entire market is relatively small so that the information only leads to non-significant portfolio revisions which hardly influence the prices. As mentioned, it shows in the considered cases that the EVI is always positive and proportional to the amount of information where the absolute risk aversion turns out to be the proportionality factor. Also for the case of incompletely known prior distributions, the corresponding information value can explicitly be determined.

As an alternative to this, secondly, the information problems within the framework of an equilibrium model is dealt with; i.e. the influence of the information process on the equilibrium prices is explicitly considered. Arbitrary groups of informed investors can be examined. Depending on whether it is assumed that the investors already realized their prior optimal portfolios before information access or nöt different information values result. For very small groups of informed investors (insiders) the results of the first approach yield as limiting case.

---

1) Philippatos, Gressis [1975] show the conformity of (μ,σ)-efficiency and (μ, entropy)-efficiency for a portfolio planning problem under the normal distribution assumption.

2) regarding entropy-approaches within the scope of this model, see Behara,Kofler, Menges [1978].

1.3 Results

For the above addressed class of information systems and the described decision scenarios, in the following, explicit formulas for the expected value of information are quoted. These ones can be numerically handled without difficulties, i.e. knowing the prior data of the decision problem and the likelihood function of the information system the EVI can immediately be evaluated without solving additional optimization problems.

For the derivation of these results the above made assumptions - in partucular, the hybrid model presumption and the normality of the information systems - are essential. From these quantitative results, however, the following, relatively plausible, qualitative and, hence, weaker statements can be concluded which also should remain valid if the assumptions are insignificantly violated and which are available to an empirical examination.

The following first four items refer to the case that the portfolio changes caused by the information activity are so insignificant that their influence on the prices at the beginning of the period can be neglected. This situation is given if the eventually informed investors are a relatively small group.[1]

- The expected value of information is always positive. Only in the merely theoretically interesting limiting case of a prior perfectly informed investor or a useless[2] information system the value zero results.
- The expected value of information is proportional to the inverse absolute risk aversion. The more risk averse an investor is, the lower he evaluates an information system. This at first sight perhaps unplausible result can be explained from that the amount riskily invested is also proportional to the inverse risk aversion. In the limiting case of an infinite risk aversion the investor always invests his whole initial wealth without any risk, and is correspondingly not interested in information about the

---

[1] i.e. the risk aversion of the group in very big, compared with the risk aversion of the entire market.

[2] the estimation variances are infinitely big.

risky assets.[1] Assuming in a first approximation that the initial wealth is also proportional to the inverse risk aversion, then as a plausible result yields that the value of an information system for an investor is a fixed fraction of his initial wealth.

- The expected value of information does not depend on the prior expectation vector of the end-of-period prices. With constant estimation accuracy, the information value does not depend for example on the condition of the market. This result can only be explained admitting short sales which enable a speculation 'à la baisse'.
- With growing prior uncertainty,[2] the information value increases. Already relatively well informed investors evaluate additional information less. This can lead to a certain assimilation of the levels of information in course of time.

Considering the information dependent changes of the prices, then it shows at first that these are also proportional to the inverse risk aversion[3] in a first approximation. The above quoted results correspondingly yield as limiting case. In addition, it results:

- The information value for an investor usually decreases, if the number of informed investors increases. It can indeed also rise, namely, if the informed group is already very big, and if the considered investor is prior better informed than the market average. In this case, the publishing of information free of charge is reasonable for the investor.
- The information value is always non-negative, if the investor already keeps his prior optimal portfolio at the information instant. The information can be worthless. This is , especially, the case if all investors have prior homogeneous expectations and all will be informed.[4]

---

[1] so far the information is not 'perfect', i.e. so far is does not completely eliminate the risk.

[2] i.e. if adding a positive definite matrix to the prior covariance matrix.

[3] of the group of the informed investors.

[4] This is the situation of an information efficient market.

- If, on the opposite to this the investor has not yet riskily invested his money at the moment of making the information decision, then a smaller information value results.[1] This one can also be negative which is, in particular, valid for homogeneous expectations and published information. Usually, it does not pay firstly to expect public information before realizing a portfolio decision, also if it is available free of charge.

1.4 Literature Survey for the Treatment of the Information Evaluation Problems in the Capital Market Theory

Although the portfolio planning has been conceived as a decision theoretic problem for more than 30 years, and although the information processing and evaluation has occupied a significant place in decision theory for a long while, there are only relatively few papers about the here treated topic of information evaluation - compared with the moreover vast number of publications about problems of capital market theory. The concerned contributions can roughly be contributed to three areas:

- information efficiency
- information processing
- information evaluation

where single papers refer to some of these areas. Further, there can be differentiated in all branches between theoretically and practically-empirically orientated papers.

In an information-efficient capital market, the equilibrium prices reflect the whole relevant information. The connection to the here treated information value problems consists in that assuming information efficiency, it cannot rationally be justified to spend money for information, because this one is already published by the complimentary observable prices in a relevant extent. Information, therefore, has no positive value. In fact, this is always true under strong efficiency and under weak efficiency in any case still for published information. If only efficient markets are

---

[1] This corresponds to the experience that the demand for corporate information for example increases after the (first) acquisition of a stock-portfolio.

considered or if one succeeds in sufficiently, empirically proofing the efficiency of real markets,[1] then information value considerations are superfluous. The then present irrelevance of such considerations becomes still clearer, if the above quoted assumptions which characterize an efficient market are considered. If the entire information is complimentarily available to all investors, then there is not only not an information value problem, but not at all an information problem (as decision problem) in itself. The equilibrium prices only then reflect the complete information, if each investor is always fully informed. If an investor asks himself whether he relies on the 'correctness' of the market prices, or whether he firstly procures information unknown to him and considered relevant, then, by this, information efficiency in the strict senseof the word is already excluded. Grossmann [1976] in this connexion comes to the result that there is no information equilibrium in an information efficient, perfect market (see also Grossmann [1978]). Presented in abridged form Grossmann arguements that it is better to renounce on a (not complimentary) information, because it can be gathered from the equilibrium prices.[2] If, however, no investor observes the information, then the information procurement again pays. None of the two situations, therefore, is stable.[3] Hellwig [1980] critizes this argumentation for good

---

1) The empirical verifications are of statistical character, i.e. it is tested because of the historical development of share-prices, whether certain, defined investment strategies supply on average significantly better results than the market portfolio. Corresponding to the asymmetric character of statistical tests, there is, strictly speaking, possible only a rejection or non-rejection, but no 'proof' of the efficiency hypothesis. While the American investigations (see Jensen [1969], Fama [1970]) support the efficiency hypothesis, Hockmann [1979] comes to opposite results for the German stock market. To the problems of efficiency tests of the market portfolio see Roll [1977] who shows that the CAPM cannot be tested for the case of inhomogeneous expectations.

2) In the special hybrid model considered by him the equilibrium price vector proves as a sufficient statistic.

3) These disequilibrium problems can only be avoided assuming certain market imperfections like uncertainty about the aggregate supply of risky assets, see Grossmann, Stiglitz [1980], Diamond, Verreccia [1981], Andersen [1983] who investigates price and quantity signals.

reasons. The equilibrium prices are results of information processes. Observing the equilibrium prices, there can only be concluded back to the own information, because one already knows this one. Hellwig avoids these difficulties by presuming a very big (infinite) market in which the single investor cannot influence the prices. This corresponds to the portfolio approach firstly examined here.

An evaluation of information in a pragmatic sense is not possible without analyzing the information processing, i.e. the influence of information on decision making. Within the scope of this book, only well defined information systems are considered the use of which the investor can freely decide. An evaluation of unsystematic, unforeseen appearing information is not possible and also not meaningful, because no information-decision problem exists.[1)] The processing of information and, hence, its influence on the investment decision are here first of all described by Bayes' theorem. This so-called Bayes approach is mainly proposed in the literature as information processing concept.[2)] Thus, Kanodia [1980] investigates the informational influence of accounting systems on the equilibrium prices and the company policies within the framework of a simultaneous, dynamic approach. By this, proposals for the dividend politics (smoothing) result.[3)]

---

1) see Jensen [1969]. Fama, Laffer [1971] and Hirshleifer [1971] distinguish in this connexion between (systematic) foreknowledge and (unsystematic) discovery.

2) Different approaches are chosen by Copeland [1976] who assumes that the demand functions are shifted by a fixed value through the information, namely upwards for optimists and downwards for pessimists, or by Jennings, Starks, Fellingham [1981] who propose a similar model for the information dependent change of the expected prices. Using game theoretic approaches Heinkel [1982] examines information spreaded by insiders for the purpose of increasing the company value. Bühler [1977] examines portfolio planning under partial information.

3) See Schnabel [1981], Spremann, Bamberg [1981]. Empirical investigations, however, attribute only a low information value to dividends and, in particular, to their change. The small improvement of the investment result caused by considering the dividend information is even overcompensated by the real transaction costs, see Watts [1973]. Möller [1983] comes to similar results for the German stock market and accounting information systems.

In many papers it is assumed that not the true end-of-period prices, as presumed here, but the expectation vector and the covariance matrix are the unknown parameters of the decision problem.[1] A summarizing representation of this approach can be found in the book of Bawa, Brown, and Klein [1979]. In particular, it is shown that a sole use of the (point) estimations for the expectations and variances as decision basis without considering the estimation risk can lead to unsatisfactory results.[2] Under suitable stationarity conditions the (prior) distribution of the prices can be estimated from past data. Some papers[3] work at special questions in this model approach and, in particular analyze the processing of (additional) information in form of further price realizations which are interpreted as a sample. Such information systems are also considered here, where the closest connexions exist with the work of Jennings, Barry [1983]. These assume the hybrid model and investigate the problem area information dissemination and speculation. They show that insiders who have an information advantage and know that this information will generally succeed in course of time should not realize an intertemporary equilibrium optimum, but speculate against the future price changes to be expected.[4] It is shown that speculation works like decreasing the risk aversion. The situation becomes more complicated if the investor after having accessed the information does not know whether he is an insider or not. It can be shown that speculation is still advantageous under this additional uncertainty if it is advantageous under certainty.[5]

---

1) This approach seems to be problematic from the decision theoretic point of view, because not the result but only a probability distribution of the possible results is determined by the made decision and the true state. Introducing hyper parameters in a hierarchical model, this approach however can be reduced to a usual Bayes decision problem (see Goel, DeGroot [1981], Goel [1983]).

2) This proceeding is often assumed implicitly, although the disadvantages of the solution of an equivalent expectation problem are generally known in the stochastic optimization theory, see for example Faber [1970], Rembold [1977].

3) Mao, Särndal [1966], Kalymon [1971], Barry [1974], Winkler, Barry [1975], Owen, Rabinovitch [1980], Lin [1981], Lin, Boot [1982], Jennings, Barry [1983].

4) The publication of insider information can be advantageous, see also Fama, Laffer [1971], Hirshleifer [1971], Sachman [1975] and sec. 1.3.

5) i.e. if the investor knows for sure that he is an insider.

The third group of papers works at the real problem of information evaluation. In analogy to the classification in portfolio models and equilibrium approaches made here, also the publications about this problems can be partitioned. The papers of Jakob, Smith [1972], Baron [1974], Morris [1974], Ohlson [1975], Merton [1981] belong to the first group which starts from exogeneously given, fixed prices at the beginning of the period. Only the paper of Jakob, Smith [1972] is an empirical investigation. The results of certain information strategies are simulated, and their profitability is examined using historical data. Baron [1974] shows the positiveness of the information value in a theoretic model. For the special information system which supplies the correct[1] message whether stocks will earn a higher return than bonds or not, Merton [1981] shows that the information value increases with the length of the forecast period and the risk tolerance. This connexion between information value and risk tolerance or - reciprocal to this - risk aversion corresponds to the results deducted here.[2] Ohlsen [1975] shows the same functional relation. For a relatively general, discrete model, he derives an index interpretable as information value which describes the profitability of an information system in comparison with a different one. This index, in any case, cannot be directly compared with the information values derived here, because, on the one hand, only discrete information systems are considered, on the other hand, only limit-statements are made which can only be analyzed for period lengths converging toward zero. Although an explicit formula is specified for the information value, this formula, hence, is numerically only hard to evaluate. Morris [1974] also determines explicitly the expected value of information, namely for the case of a logarithmic utility function and assuming that only lending and no borrowing is allowed. It shows that under these assumptions the expected value of information is proportional to the initial wealth. As the made presumptions are very essential for deriving the results, a reference to the hybrid model approach chosen here and to the results yielding from this is not directly given.

---

1) Not necessarily perfect forecasts are examined, too.

2) see sec. 1.3, Helling [1980] shows in the hybrid model the same relation between informational affected changes of the equilibrium prices and the risk aversion.

The second group of papers on the information value problem which consider the influence of information on the equilibrium prices, only present qualitative results. This is not astonishing, because it is started from much more general models which, correspondingly, do not allow an explicit information value determination. Only Fama, Laffer [1971] propose for one risky asset assuming risk neutrality an explicitly determinable information value which is proportional to the expected absolute price change. This value only measures the profits of an insider speculation; it is intuitively motivated, but not derived within a decision theoretic model.

Starting from the paper of Fama, Laffer [1971] who because of game theoretic considerations come to the result that published information cannot be worth for the group of investors as a whole, some authors investigate these problems more precisely. The contributions of Hirshleifer [1971], Jaffe [1975], Hakansson, Kunkel, Ohlson [1982], and Kunkel [1982] verify under different assumptions that published information, in any case, then have no negative value, if prior the optimal portfoliosare kept. If the market is inefficient in the sense that the investors have inhomogeneous expectations or start from different likelihood functions, then even a positive value yields - in accordance with the results deducted here. Hirshleifer [1971] shows for the case of homogeneous expectations and for a world of pure exchange that information which is worthless if published has a positive value for insiders. Similar to Owen, Rabinovitch [1978], it results that a subsequent publication of the insider information sill reinforces this positive information effect (from the insider's point of view).

Finally, it should still be pointed at the very interesting paper of Wahl [1983]. He deals with the information value problems as well assuming fixed prices as in an equilibrium model. A two-periodic, integrated investment and consumption model is examined. All considered random variables are discrete, i.e. only a finite set of price developments and a finite set of pieces of information are though possible. The investors have logarithmic utility functions, and, usually, inhomogeneous expectations. Only the two cases are considered that solely one investor (insider information) or all market participants (published information) are informed. Wahl defines the information value as (expected) utility increase if explicitly considering the information costs. This definition is problematic, because utility functions are uniquely defined only up to positive, linear transformations. Strictly speaking, with the aid of this information value, only qualitative statements are possible: The sign decides about the profitability of an information activity. A further disadvantage of this approach is that the information costs have to be explicitly known while here the maximum tolerable information cost are determined. In spitè of the different model approaches and the different information value definitions, partly comparable results yield. In particular, Wahl also derives a positive information value for insiders, if no information costs come into existence, and a proportionality between the information value and the amount of information. This last result is not surprising because of the assumed, logarithmic utility function, see Kelly [1956].

Summarizing, it can be stated that - different from the results concluded here - in the literature, leaving aside the papers of Morris [1974], Ohlson [1975], and Wahl [1983] only qualitative results are presented. The formulas specified in those three papers are numerically only hard to evaluate (Ohlson) or are only in a limited way comparable to the results concluded here because of the different model approach (Morris, Wahl).

2. Information Processing and Information Evaluation without Considering the Information Effected Price Changes: The Portfolio Approach

In this section, it is assumed that the asset prices at the beginning of the period are exogeneously given and are not influenced by the changes of the information level. There are no market considerations. Correspondingly, it is insignificant here whether the prices are equilibrium prices or not. In the third section, then, information dependent price changes in a market equilibrium model are examined. In order to simplify comparing the results of these two sections, a model formulation is already chosen here that starts from the prices, and not as usual from the rates of return. This one is more suitable for describing and analyzing the market equilibria at different information levels as examined in the third section. This becomes clear, if one considers that an information dependent change of the expectations of the end-of-period asset prices influences their stochastic rates of return (more precisely: the expectations of these rates of return) in twofold manner. Besides the stochastic, information dependent influence of the distribution of the end-of-period prices on the rate of return distribution, namely, a systematic change of the rate of return by the change of the equilibrium prices is still to be taken into account.

2.1 The Hybrid Model

In the following, the *hybrid model* so designated under the influence of Bamberg, Spremann [1981] is considered. It is characterized by two relatively restrictive assumptions: The considered decision-maker starts prior from multidimensional normally distributed end-of-period values[1] and has an exponential utility function, i.e. a constant absolute risk aversion.[2]

---

[1] The hybrid model can also be assumed for general, decision theoretic problems. The term 'end-of-period prices' is then to by replaced by 'state parameter'. Surely, the hybrid model is especially tailored for the case of a result function linear in the state parameters which is then also normally distributed for each fixed chosen decision.

[2] Regarding the meaning of the absolute risk aversion, see Pratt [1964], Arrow [1965]. Amihud [1980] proposes a generalization of this risk aversion measure.

Hence, it is started with an investor (decision-maker), whose utility function which is defined on a real result g of a decision is given by

$$(1) \qquad u(g) = -e^{-\alpha g} \qquad \forall\, g \in \mathbb{R} .$$

The real number $\alpha > 0$ is the *constant absolute risk aversion* independent of the special result,

$$\alpha = -\frac{u''(g)}{u'(g)} \qquad \forall\, g \in \mathbb{R} .$$

The investor endowed with the initial wealth $w \in \mathbb{R}$ [1] is offered within the scope of a one periodic portfolio planning problem a total of n risky assets. The vectors of the prices at the beginning of the period, respectively the end-of-period prices are designated by v respectively X :

$$v = (v_1,\ldots,v_n)^T$$
$$X = (X_1,\ldots,X_n)^T .$$

In order to avoid the here unnecessary introduction of an additional variable, namely of the vector of the number of shares of the single assets, the components of v and X are conceived as total values, i.e. v_i , respectively X_i specifies the value (price) of asset i in total at the beginning respectively end of the period.

While $v \in \mathbb{R}^n$ is supposed to be given exogeneously and to be known to the decision-maker, the end-of-period values X are unknown at the beginning of the period. X is, correspondingly, interpreted as n-dimensional random variable. The realization of X , i.e. the actual, only ex post known price vector at the end of the period is designated by x . The investor defines his pre-knowledge by a prior distribution of X , described by a density φ . It is presupposed that the prices X are evaluated by the investor as *prior normally distributed* with expectation vector $\mu \in \mathbb{R}^n$, and positive definite covariance matrix $\Omega \in \mathbb{R}^{(n,n)}$:

$$(2) \qquad X \sim N(\mu,\Omega) .$$

φ is, therefore, the density of an $N(\mu,\Omega)$-distribution.

---

[1] also negative values are admitted.

Let the portfolio vector chosen by the investor be

$$y = (y_1, \ldots, y_n)^T \in \mathbb{R}^n ,$$

where y_i denotes the fraction of the asset i which the investor holds.[1] *The end-of-period wealth* then yields as result of the decision and depends on the end-of-period values under the assumptions of a perfect capital market as described in section 1.1:

(3) $$g(x,y) = (w - \sum_{j=1}^{n} y_j v_j)(1+r) + \sum_{j=1}^{n} y_j x_j$$

$$= w(1+r) + y^T(x - (1+r)v) \quad \forall\, x,y \in \mathbb{R}^n ;$$

r stands for the risk free interest rate at which any amount can be borrowed or saved. According to (2), also negative components are admitted for x. This is only hard or not at all to interpret because of the given limited liability of stockholders. If the expectations and variances of the asset prices have a realistic relation, then the probability for the occurrence of negative prices, however, is small and can be neglected.

In the scope of a decision theoretic approach as the hybrid model represents it, the evaluation of a decision - here y - is made corresponding to the Bayes-principle by the expected utility or by the certainty equivalent of the result - here g. Designating the density of the distribution of the state parameters - here x - by ψ [2], then the *certainty equivalent* of the decision y is defined as:

(4) $$\upsilon_\psi(g(X,y)) = u^{-1}(E_\psi\, u(g(X,y))) .$$

Let ψ, in the following, always be the density of a normal distribution. As g according to (3) is a linear function in x, $g(X,y)$ is also normally distributed, if $y \neq 0$.[3]

In this case, the determination of υ_ψ is particularly simple:[4]

---

1) Normally, $0 \leq y_i \leq 1$; negative components of y correspond to short sales and components greater than one to a 'corner'.

2) Prior $\varphi = \psi$, i.e. according to (2) ψ prior is the density of an $N(\mu,\Omega)$-distribution. In the following, however, also posterior distributions are considered, i.e. ψ can also describe the changed expectations after information access.

3) Yet, all following statements are also valid analogously for $y = 0$.

4) See Pratt, Raiffa, Schlaifer [1965], Bamberg, Spremann [1981].

$$(5) \qquad \upsilon_{\psi}(g(X,y)) = E_{\psi}\, g(X,y) - \frac{\alpha}{2} \mathrm{Var}_{\psi}\, g(X,y)$$

$$= w(1+r) + y^T(E_{\psi}\, X - (1+r)v) - \frac{\alpha}{2} y^T(\mathrm{Cov}_{\psi}\, X)y \; .$$

According to (2), prior especially the following is true:

$$(6) \qquad \upsilon_{\varphi}(g(X,y)) = w(1+r) + y^T(\mu - (1+r)v) - \frac{\alpha}{2} y^T \Omega y$$

It follows immediately from (1) and (4) that υ_{ψ} is linear[1] with regard to an additive constant:

$$\upsilon_{\psi}(g(X,y) + c) = \upsilon_{\psi}(g(X,y)) + c \qquad \forall\, c \in \mathbb{R}$$

According to Pfanzagl [1959], this consistence condition uniquely characterizes the class of the utility functions with constant absolute risk aversion.[2] According to (5) or (6), the optimal decision, therefore, the optimal portfolio y^*, then is independent of the initial wealth w. This property following directly from the consistence condition and, therefore, characterizing for the hybrid model contradicts to practical experiences and, hence, gives occasion to criticism.[3] On the other hand, Pfanzagl [1959] points at the difficulties which oppose to each experimental utility determination, if the consistence condition is missing. Determining the utility for a decider without precisely defining his wealth situation then, namely, is not possible.

According to (5), the certainty equivalent only depends on the expectation and on the variance of the end-of-period wealth:

$$(7) \qquad \upsilon_{\psi}(g(X,y)) = K(E_{\psi}\, g(X,y), \mathrm{Var}_{\psi}\, g(X,y))$$

This is not surprising, because $g(X,y)$ is normally distributed and the normal distributions form a (μ,σ)-class.[4]

As a necessary optimality condition,[5], hence, it yields[6]

---

1) The assumption of a normal distribution is not required for this.

2) where linear utility functions - they have a risk aversion $\alpha = 0$ - are included; for weakening this consistence condition to a local condition which also uniquely characterizes the utility functions with constant absolute risk aversion, see Bamberg, Spremann [1981],[1983].

3) see for example Sinn [1980], Bitz [1981].

4) see Schneeweiß [1967].

5) under suitable, here fulfilled regularity conditions.

6) K_i is the partial derivative of K with respect to the i-th component.

$$0 = K_1(E_\psi\, g(X,y^*), Var_\psi\, g(X,y^*)) \cdot \frac{d\, E_\psi\, g(X,y)}{dy}(y^*)$$

$$+ K_2(E_\psi\, g(X,y^*), Var_\psi\, g(X,y^*)) \cdot \frac{d\, Var_\psi\, g(X,y)}{dy}(y^*)$$

According to (3), the following is true

$$\frac{d\, E_\psi\, g(X,y)}{dy} = E_\psi\, X - (1+r)v$$

$$\frac{d\, Var_\psi\, g(X,y)}{dy} = 2(Cov_\psi\, X) \cdot y$$

and, hence:[1]

(8) $$y^* = -\frac{K_1(y^*)}{2K_2(y^*)} (Cov_\psi\, X)^{-1}(E_\psi\, X - (1+r)v)$$

Under the assumptions of the hybrid model, (8) is an explicit solution of this problem, for according to (5),(7), the following is true:

$$K_1(y^*) = 1 \;,\quad K_2(y^*) = -\frac{\alpha}{2}$$

and, hence

(9) $$y^* = \frac{1}{\alpha} (Cov_\psi\, X)^{-1}(E_\psi\, X - (1+r)v) \;.$$

According to (2), prior especially

(10) $$y^* = \frac{1}{\alpha} \Omega^{-1}(\mu - (1+r)v)$$

holds. According to (5)

(11) $$\max_{y \in \mathbb{R}^n} v_\psi(g(X,y)) = v_\psi(g(X,y^*))$$

$$= w(1+r) + \frac{1}{2\alpha}(E_\psi\, X - (1+r)v)^T (Cov_\psi\, X)^{-1}(E_\psi\, X - (1+r)v)$$

results as optimal value of the objective function, i.e. as maximum certainty equivalent, and prior especially

(12) $$v_\varphi(g(X,y^*)) = w(1+r) + \frac{1}{2\alpha}(\mu - (1+r)v)^T \Omega^{-1}(\mu - (1+r)v) \;.$$

By (10) and (12), the portfolio planning problem is completely solved for a fixed information level within the framework of the hybrid

---

[1] $Cov_\psi X$ is assumed to be positive definite; as an abbreviation $K_i(y^*) = K_i(E_\psi\, g(X,y^*), Var_\psi\, g(X,y^*))$ is written $(i = 1,2)$.

model. As Ω is positive definite, y^* is also the only solution of the optimization problem.

(9) and (10) can, of course, also be derived directly from (5) and (6). The way chosen here has the advantage that it enables uniquely characterizing the hybrid model. Epps [1981] showed that only the hybrid model has the property that the underlying utility function[1] leads to a (μ,σ)-rule and, simultaneously, (8) specifies an explicit solution of the portfolio problem for arbitrary r,[2] w,v, i.e. $K_1/2K_2$ is a constant independent of the made decision.[3] While the consistence condition uniquely characterizes only one presumption of the hybrid model, namely the presumption of a constant risk aversion, Epps [1981], therefore, specifies necessary and sufficient conditions for the validity of *both* presumptions of the hybrid model. Other portfolio models which underly a (μ,σ)-rule, therefore, have to hurt the condition that (8) represents an explicit solution of the decision problem. If $K_1/2K_2$ then depends in a simple way on the decision, y^* can explicitly be determined from (8).[4] Generally such an explicit solution of the problem, however, is no longer possible.

According to (9) and (10), the composition of the optimal portfolio is independent of α and w. The risk attitude of the investor only influences the total amount to be invested riskily. In order to show this property which is denoted *separation*, it is already sufficient to presume one of the two assumptions of the hybrid model.[5]

Determining the optimal portfolio, i.e. the decision y^*, which maximizes $\upsilon_\phi(g(X,y))$, v is considered to be constant. This corresponds to the assumption that the investors are price-takers which is characteristic for a perfect capital market (see section 1.1). Also if, in the following, it is started from variable information levels and equilibrium prices dependent on them, it is always assumed that the optimization of the portfolio decision is performed

---

[1] only twice differentiable, strictly monotonously increasing, strictly concave utility functions are considered which presents no essential limitation for the presumed portfolio problem.

[2] The existence of a risk free asset is essential for the validity of the statement.

[3] Epps [1981] sets up another requirement for the second derivatives which is unnecessary according to Bamberg [1983].

[4] see Bamberg [1983].

[5] see Cass, Stiglitz [1970], Ross [1978], Bamberg, Spremann [1981], Dybvig, Ingersoll jr. [1982], Chamberlain [1983], Franke [1983].

at fixed prices. The information activity might change the expectations of the investors and, hence, the equilibrium prices. The optimal portfolio, however, is determined at these fixed, new prices. This assumption is problematic in particular, if the investor possesses (almost) perfect knowledge about the end-of-period prices ($\Omega \approx 0$, see (10)). The hybrid model presented here supplies in this case no convincing description of the reality. Indeed, the information levels of the investors are usually in reality extremly imperfect. Bus also then this price-taker assumption is a problem. In particular, if the market directly after new information access is not in equilibrium.[1)]

In the literature, the distribution type of the end-of-period prices is a point of controversy. While for example Jensen [1969] assumes a stable distribution with infinite variance because of empirical investigations, Mossin [1973] does not at all regard the normal distribution assumption empirically to be a problem. All these approaches start from objective and correspondingly, homogeneous expectations while here a subjective probability concept is assumed. How the prices are, in fact, distributed and how they are distributed in the opinion of the investors, are two different questions. If the true distribution of the prices were known to the investor, then he should conveniently base his decisions on it.[2)] But a sufficiently precise estimation of this distribution even under very problematic stationarity assumptions is only possible with big effort,[3)] and, correspondingly, is not attempted by the majority of investors in reality.

Generalizations and extensions of the hybrid model are possible in different ways. Thus in the following section, the requirement of perfect knowledge of the prior distribution is weakened. Another possibility here not further investigated is the consideration of multi-periodic problems.So Mossin [1968] examines among other things

---

1) see Rudolph [1982], Spremann, Bamberg [1983a], who examine monopolistic behavior.

2) see section 2.2.2 .

3) Levy, Kroll [1980], Maier, Peterson, Van der Weide [1982] point at the big number of periods to be considered. Jobson, Korkie [1980] (James-Stein-estimator) and Cohen, Hawawini, Maier, Schwartz, Whitcomb [1983] propose improvements of the classical least squares estimators. To the consideration of non-stationarity processes by estimating the 'shift', see Hsu [1982].

optimal myopic politics under the assumption of constant absolute risk aversion. Usually, such models lead to a dynamic optimization problem.[1]

2.2 Extensions of the Hybrid Model for the Case of Not Completely Known Prior Data

Assuming the hybrid model for the portfolio planning problem - besides α, v and r - the prior data μ and Ω have to be known to determine the optimal portfolio (see (10)). It was already pointed at the difficulties to determine the price distribution, if assuming an objective concept of probability. But also within the scope of the subjective approach represented here the investor can be demanded too much specifying μ and Ω. If the investor does not have any information about μ and Ω,[2] then the decision problem is only meaningfully solvable applying the Minimax-rule by $y^* = 0$. The investor then invests his whole initial wealth without any risk and receives a secure end-of-period wealth $w(1+r)$.

The assumption of certain preinformation about μ and Ω leads to more interesting results. In the following, two alternative scenarios are considered. First (section 2.2.1 and 2.2.2), two solution possibilities are discussed for a *risk situation* with regard to the prior parameters.[3] In Sec. 2.2.3, the case of partial *uncertainty* about μ and Ω is treated. This also leads to the problem not further examined here how - in the sense of a sensitivity analysis - the precision of the determination of the prior data influences the portfolio decision and also the information evaluation.[4]

---

[1] see Goldwerger [1977].

[2] i.e. the onle preinformation is that the end-of-period prices are normally distributed.

[3] Only risk situations with regard to μ are investigated. The represented two-level risk approaches are usually interpreted in a combined subjective-objective way: There is an objective, but not completely known distribution of the prices on whose parameters subjective expectations exist, see the literature specified in Sec. 2.2.1, 2.2.2 .

[4] Regarding the influence of the precision of prior data on the expected value of information within the framework of a general discrete decision model, see Firchau [1980b].

2.2.1 Risk Situation with Regard to the Prior Parameters: A Two-Level Bayes Approach

The description of the portfolio planning problem presented here is not the only possibility to formulate the problem as decision problem under risk. Besides the state-preference-approach,[1] especially those approaches are to be mentioned which do not consider - as in Section 2.1 - the prior parameters μ and Ω as known variables, but as the true unknown environment parameters.[2] Usually it is assumed that the investor determines a prior distribution of the parameters (μ,Ω) .[3] As also with sure knowledge of μ and Ω the end-of-period values and, therefore, the end-of-period wealth are still not known by sure, it concerns a two-level, hierarchical problem with (μ,Ω) as hyperparameter.[4] Such an approach is, of course, in principle not limited to two levels. Concerning the problems of information-processing and -evaluation for general hierarchical decision models and different uncertainty functions see Goel, DeGroot [1981], Goel [1983].

In this section, it is assumed that the two-level problem is reduced to a usual one-level decision problem through the formula for the total probability. Presuming only uncertainty about μ , defined in detail by a prior normal distribution, this problem can be reduced to the problem within the scope of the hybrid model:

<u>Theorem 1:</u>

Given are $m \in \mathbb{R}^n$ and positive definite matrices $\Pi,\Omega \in \mathbb{R}^{(n,n)}$. Let M be an $N(m,\Pi)$-distributed random variable:

(13) $$M \sim N(m,\Pi) .$$

Under the condition '$M=\mu$' let X be $N(\mu,\Omega)$-distributed:

(14) $$X|_{M=\mu} \sim N(\mu,\Omega) \quad \forall\ \mu \in \mathbb{R}^n ,$$

then the marginal (unconditional) distribution of X is an $N(m,\Omega+\Pi)$-distribution:

---

1) see for example Morris [1974], Wilhelm [1981].

2) see for example Mao, Särndal [1966], Kalymon [1971], Barry [1974], Winkler, Barry [1975], Jennings, Barry [1983] and, especially, the book from Bawa, Brown, Klein [1979] which summarizes the early papers of the authors.

3) Uncertainty approaches are dealt with in section 2.2.3 .

4) I.e. a parameter which determines the 'true' prior distribution.

(15) $X \sim N(m, \Omega + \Pi)$.

Theorem 1 is a standard statement about normal distributions. A proof is for example found in LaValle [1970].

(13) and (14) describe the underlying two-level decision problem. The investor has an $N(\mu,\Omega)$-distribution as a prior distribution (see section (2)) where he only knows Ω precisely, and about μ a prior distribution on a higher level according to (13) is known. This two-level problem can be reduced to a one-level one according to (15). For the investor, X is, therefore, 'actually' prior $N(m,\Omega+\Pi)$-distributed. He knows the parameters of this distribution. Hence, the problem is reduced to a problem which can be treated within the scope of the hybrid model approach.

Also if - as in the specified literature - the two-level problem is interpreted in a combined objective-subjective way,[1] (15) does represent a distribution which can only be interpreted subjectively. This becomes especially clear by considering the covariances. If X is actually $N(\mu,\Omega)$-distributed and if Ω is known, then an as good as possible approximation of this objective distribution should anyway estimate the covariance by Ω . Conversely, the covariance matrix of X according to (15) is $\Omega + \Pi$, i.e. the prior distribution (15) of X still considers besides Ω the subjective estimation risk of the estimation of μ .[2]

Within the scope of this two-level model approach it would be in itself desirable to also treat risk situations with regard to Ω . Here, however, it is renounced on this, because the marginal distribution of X then usually[3] is not a normal distribution, i.e. the corresponding one-level problem can no longer be treated within the scope of the hybrid model.

---

1) hence, the distributions in (13) are considered as subjective and in (14) as objective.

2) Regarding the significance of the estimation risk at the estimation of the decision parameters see Bawa, Brown, Klein [1979].

3) The marginal distribution of X , of course, depends on the presupposed prior distribution for Ω . Similarly simple results as theorem 1 are not to be expected or only for special cases, because the prior distribution is to be defined on the very complex set of all positive definite matrices, provided with a suitable σ-algebra.

Assuming a constant absolute risk aversion α (see (1)) and the risk situation described in theorem 1 for the investor, then his portfolio decision problem can be solved according to section 2.1 . In the corresponding formulas, only μ has to be replaced by m and Ω by $\Omega + \Pi$:[1]

$$(16) \qquad \tilde{y}^* = \frac{1}{\alpha}(\Omega+\Pi)^{-1}(m - (1+r)v)$$

$$(17) \qquad \upsilon_{\tilde{\varphi}}(g(X,\tilde{y}^*)) = w(1+r) + \frac{1}{2\alpha}(m - (1+r)v)^T(\Omega+\Pi)^{-1}(m - (1+r)v)$$

The variance of the end-of-period wealth depending on an arbitrary portfolio decision y , is (see (3),(5),(6))

$$(18) \qquad \mathrm{Var}_{\tilde{\varphi}}\, g(X,y) = y^T(\Omega+\Pi)y \ .$$

As Π,Ω are positive definite, the following is true (see (163)):

$$\mathrm{Var}_{\tilde{\varphi}}\, g(X,y) > y^T\Omega y = \mathrm{Var}_{\varphi}\, g(X,y)$$

Additional uncertainty about μ , hence, leads for the same portfolio decision to a bigger variance of the end-of-period wealth, i.e. to a higher risk. It will show that this also leads to an increase of the information value.

2.2.2 Risk Situation with Regard to the Prior Parameters: Lin's Approach

Lin [1981] proposes an alternative possibility of solving the two-level decision problem under risk presented in Sec. 2.2.1.[2] In Sec. 2.2.1, the distributions were aggregated by the formula of the total probability to an adequate subjective prior distribution. Conversely, within the scope of Lin's approach it is tried to subjectively estimate the objectively right but not completely known distribution of the end-of-period values. The result is, accordingly, indeed subjectively influenced, but has the character of an objective distribution. The approach, therefore, stands in a certain opposition to the subjective standpoint represented here and is no

---

1) $\tilde{\varphi}$ here stands for an $N(m,\Omega+\Pi)$-distribution, therefore, for the 'true' prior distribution. Analogously, $\tilde{y}^*$ denotes the optimal portfolio with regard to the prior distribution $\tilde{\varphi}$.

2) see also Lin, Boot [1982].

longer considered, in the following. A short representation of the characteristics of the model compared to the approach presented in Sec. 2.2.1, however, seems to be convenient.

Assume that X is $N(\mu,\Omega)$-distributed (see (2)):

$$X \sim N(\mu,\Omega) \ ,$$

and that the parameters (μ,Ω) are objectively right, but unknown. Let the investor estimate (μ,Ω) by $(\hat{\mu},\hat{\Omega})$.[1] For the evaluation of the quality of the estimation it is obvious to base on the following loss function:[2]

$$(19) \qquad L((\mu,\Omega),(\hat{\mu},\hat{\Omega})) = \nu_\varphi(g(X,y^*)) - \nu_\varphi(g(X,\hat{y}^*)) \ .$$

L specifies the opportunity costs - described by the certainty equivalents - at the end of the period, which result from the (wrong) estimation of (μ,Ω) by $(\hat{\mu},\hat{\Omega})$ and the thereby caused (wrong) decision $\hat{y}^*$. Obviously it holds:

$$L((\mu,\Omega),(\hat{\mu},\hat{\Omega})) \geq 0$$
$$L((\mu,\Omega),(\mu,\Omega)) = 0 \ ,$$

i.e. knowing the objectively right distribution this one is meaningfully based at decision making.

According to (9), the following is true:

$$\hat{y}^* = \frac{1}{\alpha}\hat{\Omega}^{-1}(\hat{\mu} - (1+r)v)$$

and, hence, according to (5),(12):

$$(20) \qquad L((\mu,\Omega),(\hat{\mu},\hat{\Omega})) = \frac{1}{2\alpha}(\mu - (1+r)v)^T\Omega^{-1}(\mu - (1+r)v)$$
$$- \frac{1}{\alpha}(\hat{\mu} - (1+r)v)^T\hat{\Omega}^{-1}(\mu - (1+r)v)$$
$$+ \frac{1}{2\alpha}(\hat{\mu} - (1+r)v)^T\hat{\Omega}^{-1}\Omega\hat{\Omega}^{-1}(\hat{\mu} - (1+r)v) \ .$$

If a prior distribution for (μ,Ω) is given, then the estimation of (μ,Ω) has to be done in a way that the expected loss related to this prior distribution is minimal:

---

1) whereby $\hat{\Omega}$ be positive definite.

2) The optimal portfolio decision is denoted by $\hat{y}^*$, if based on an $N(\hat{\mu},\hat{\Omega})$-distribution for X. Again φ is the density of an $N(\mu,\Omega)$-distribution.

$$EL((\mu,\Omega),(\hat{\mu}^*,\hat{\Omega}^*)) = \min_{(\hat{\mu},\hat{\Omega})} EL((\mu,\Omega),(\hat{\mu},\hat{\Omega})) \ .$$

Here the expectations have to be formed with regard to the prior distribution of (μ,Ω). For the situation described in theorem 1, i.e. for the case that Ω is known and μ is prior $N(m,\Pi)$-distributed, it holds according to (20) (see (171)):

(21) $$EL((\mu,\Omega),(\hat{\mu},\hat{\Omega})) = \frac{1}{2\alpha}[(m-(1+r)v)^T\Omega^{-1}(m-(1+r)v)$$
$$+ tr(\Omega^{-1}\Pi)] - \frac{1}{\alpha}(\hat{\mu}-(1+r)v)^T\hat{\Omega}^{-1}(m-(1+r)v)$$
$$+ \frac{1}{2\alpha}(\hat{\mu}-(1+r)v)^T\hat{\Omega}^{-1}\Omega\hat{\Omega}^{-1}(\hat{\mu}-(1+r)v)$$
$$=: Z(\hat{\mu},\hat{\Omega}) \ .$$

Partial differentiation of Z to $\hat{\mu}$ yields:

$$\frac{\partial Z}{\partial\hat{\mu}} = -\frac{1}{\alpha}\hat{\Omega}^{-1}(m-(1+r)v) + \frac{1}{\alpha}\hat{\Omega}^{-1}\Omega\hat{\Omega}^{-1}(\hat{\mu}-(1+r)v) \ .$$

Hence, it follows as a necessary optimality condition

(22) $$\Omega^{-1}(m-(1+r)v) = \hat{\Omega}^{*-1}(\hat{\mu}^*-(1+r)v) \ .$$

(22) replaced in (21) yields:

$$Z(\hat{\mu}^*,\hat{\Omega}^*) = \frac{1}{2\alpha}[(m-(1+r)v)^T\Omega^{-1}(m-(1+r)v)$$
$$+ tr(\Omega^{-1}\Pi)] - \frac{1}{\alpha}(m-(1+r)v)^T\Omega^{-1}(m-(1+r)v)$$
$$+ \frac{1}{2\alpha}(m-(1+r)v)^T\Omega^{-1}(m-(1+r)v)$$
$$= \frac{1}{2\alpha}tr(\Omega^{-1}\Pi) \ .$$

This is no longer dependent on $(\hat{\mu}^*,\hat{\Omega}^*)$, i.e. each admissible[1] solution of (22) minimizes[2] (21). The admissible solutions of (22) obviously are:

$\hat{\Omega}^*$ arbitrary (positive definite)

$\hat{\mu}^* = \hat{\Omega}^*\Omega^{-1}(m-(1+r)v) + (1+r)v$.

---

1) $\hat{\Omega}^*$ has to be positive definite.

2) Z is continuous, non-negative and obviously has a minimum. The solutions of (22) can, therefore, only be minima.

All these solutions lead to the same optimal portfolio-decision (see (9)):

$$\hat{y}^{**} = \frac{1}{\alpha}\,\Omega^{-1}(m - (1+r)v) \; .$$

Seen from a pragmatic standpoint, a more precise determination of $(\hat{\mu}^*,\hat{\Omega}^*)$ is unnecessary. As Ω was presupposed to be objectively right and known, it is obvious to choose the special solution

$$(23) \qquad (\hat{\mu}^*,\hat{\Omega}^*) = (m,\Omega) \; .$$

A comparison with (15) shows that with the approach chosen here the covariance matrix Π need not be considered.

2.2.3 Partial Uncertainty with Regard to the Prior Parameters

Both presented risk approaches for the solution of the portfolio planning problem under uncertainty about the prior parameters have - as each risk approach - the disadvantage, to need the specification of a prior distribution for the parameters. As theorem 1 shows, the decision-maker is only apparently less demanded: The specification of a prior distribution of the second level practically means the determination of a prior distribution for the actual, underlying problem. Therefore, it is obvious to start from an uncertainty approach which demands from the decision-maker the definition of few data. For a (μ,σ)-approach this was first proposed by Bühler [1977] for the portfolio problem. Within a special index model he led the decision problem back to a vector optimization problem, see also Bühler [1984].

The approach presented here corresponds to the concept of *partial information* based on the papers of Bierlein [1963] and Richter [1963] as it was founded as linear partial information by Kofler, Menges [1976] and extended by Kofler, Menges, Fahrion, Huschens, Kuss [1980] to the concept of the stochastic partial information. However, the following model can only be filed under this concept in a limited way, because the sets of distributions considered here are (corresponding to the hybrid model) sets of normal distributions and, therefore, usually extremely non-convex.[1]

---

[1] Even the convex combination (mixture) of two normal distributions is in general no longer normal.

For the two risk approaches presented above it was assumed that the investor considers each normal distribution[1] as a prior to be possible but differently probable. Now it is presupposed that the investor only determines one class Φ of densities containing the density of the prior distribution without a more precise specification in the form of a higher level prior distribution.

In agreement to the hybrid model approach it is postulated:

Φ is non-empty and contains only densities of normal distributions.

Except in trivial special cases Φ is not convex and not a polyhedron,[2] i.e. Φ is no linear partial information in the sense of Kofler, Menges [1976]. The $\mathrm{MaxE}_{\min}$-principle (so termed by Kofler, Menges [1976]) which comprises the Bayes- und Minimax-principle as extremes is chosen as optimality criterion:[3]

(24) $$\min_{\varphi\in\Phi} E_\varphi\, u(g(X,\tilde{\tilde{y}}^*)) = \max_{y\in\mathbb{R}^n} \min_{\varphi\in\Phi} E_\varphi\, u(g(X,y))$$

or (u^{-1} is monotonously increasing):

(25) $$\min_{\varphi\in\Phi} \nu_\varphi(g(X,\tilde{\tilde{y}}^*)) = \max_{y\in\mathbb{R}^n} \min_{\varphi\in\Phi} \nu_\varphi(g(X,y)) \ .$$

Then $\tilde{\tilde{y}}^*$ is the optimal decision with respect to this criterion, and (25) specifies the corresponding certainty equivalent of this decision for the $\mathrm{MaxE}_{\min}$-principle.

As Φ only contains normal distributions, it is obvious to describe Φ by the possible (μ,Ω)-combinations:[4]

(26) $$\Theta := \{(\mu,\Omega) \mid \exists\, \varphi\in\Phi : \varphi \textit{ is the density of an } N(\mu,\Omega)\textit{-distribution}\} \ .$$

---

1) with fixed covariance matrix Ω in the considered special cases.

2) A finite union of convex polyhedrons is called polyhedron. If Φ is finite, then Φ is also a polyhedron.

3) Let Φ be such that the occurring maxima and minima exist. It will show that this is true for the special cases considered in the following.

4) Again only positive definite covariance matrices are taken into account.

To secure that $\tilde{\tilde{y}}^*$ exists and that $\tilde{\tilde{y}}^*$ and the associated certainty equivalent can easily be determined, it is sufficient to suppose θ as compact and convex.

Theorem 2:

Let the investor specify his preknowledge by a class Φ of normal distributions as possible prior distributions. Let the associated range of parameters θ according to (26) be compact and convex. Then the following is true:

$$(27) \qquad \tilde{\tilde{y}}^* = \frac{1}{\alpha} \tilde{\tilde{\Omega}}^{*-1} (\tilde{\tilde{\mu}}^* - (1+r)v)$$

is the uniquely determined optimal portfolio decision concerning the MaxE_{min}-criterion with the associated certainty equivalent:

$$(28) \qquad \min_{\varphi \in \Phi} \upsilon_\varphi (g(X,\tilde{\tilde{y}}^*)) = w(1+r) + \frac{1}{2\alpha} (\tilde{\tilde{\mu}}^* - (1+r)v)^T \tilde{\tilde{\Omega}}^{*-1} (\tilde{\tilde{\mu}}^* - (1+r)v)$$

where $(\tilde{\tilde{\mu}}^*, \tilde{\tilde{\Omega}}^*) \in \theta$ is a solution of the following optimization problem

$$(29) \qquad (\tilde{\tilde{\mu}}^* - (1+r)v)^T \tilde{\tilde{\Omega}}^{*-1} (\tilde{\tilde{\mu}}^* - (1+r)v)$$

$$= \min_{(\mu,\Omega) \in \theta} (\mu - (1+r)v)^T \Omega^{-1} (\mu - (1+r)v) \ .$$

It should be noted that from the convexity of θ, however, the convexity of Φ not at all follows.

Proof:

It follows from (6):

$$\upsilon_\varphi (g(X,y)) = w(1+r) + y^T (\mu - (1+r)v) - \frac{\alpha}{2} y^T \Omega y \ .$$

This expression is strictly concave as function of y and linear, therefore convex, as function of (μ,Ω). As θ and $\mathbb{R}^n$ are closed and convex, the following is true (see (166),(173)):

$$\inf_{\varphi \in \Phi} \sup_{y \in \mathbb{R}^n} \upsilon_\varphi (g(X,y)) = \sup_{y \in \mathbb{R}^n} \inf_{\varphi \in \Phi} \upsilon_\varphi (g(X,y)) \ .$$

Obviously the first supremum (see (11)) and the two infima are attained because the underlying functions are continuous:

$$\min_{\varphi \in \Phi} \max_{y \in \mathbb{R}^n} \upsilon_\varphi (g(X,y)) = \sup_{y \in \mathbb{R}^n} \min_{\varphi \in \Phi} \upsilon_\varphi (g(X,y))$$

Firstly, it is shown that also the second supremum is attained. Let

(μ',Ω') be an arbitrary element of Θ, then:

(30) $$Z(y) := \min_{\varphi\in\Phi} \upsilon_\varphi(g(X,y))$$

$$= \min_{(\mu,\Omega)\in\Theta} [w(1+r) + y^T(\mu - (1+r)v) - \frac{\alpha}{2} y^T \Omega y]$$

$$\leq w(1+r) + y^T(\mu' - (1+r)v) - \frac{\alpha}{2} y^T \Omega' y$$

$$\leq w(1+r) + \|y\| a - \|y\|^2 b$$

with

(31) $$\|y\| := \sqrt{y^T y}$$

(32) $$a := \max_{y:\|y\|=1} y^T(\mu' - (1+r)v)$$

(33) $$, \; b := \min_{y:\|y\|=1} \frac{\alpha}{2} y^T \Omega' y > 0$$

(31) is the definition of the usual (Euclidean) norm. The maxima and minima in (32),(33) are attained, because the considered set is compact and the corresponding functions are continuous. As Ω is always positive definite, b is positive. Then it follows from (30):

$$Z(y) < w(1+r) \quad \text{if} \quad \|y\| > \frac{|a|}{b}$$

Because of $Z(0) = w(1+r)$, therefore, Z attains its global maximum within the compact set :[1]

$$K = \{y \in \mathbb{R}^n : \|y\| \leq \frac{|a|}{b}\}$$

i.e. the following is true:

$$\sup_{y\in\mathbb{R}^n} Z(y) = \sup_{y\in K} Z(y) = \max_{y\in K} Z(y) = \max_{y\in\mathbb{R}^n} Z(y)$$

or

(34) $$\min_{\varphi\in\Phi} \max_{y\in\mathbb{R}^n} \upsilon_\varphi(g(X,y)) = \max_{y\in\mathbb{R}^n} \min_{\varphi\in\Phi} \upsilon_\varphi(g(X,y)) =: V$$

Hence, the existence of an optimal decision relating to the $MaxE_{min}$-criterion is shown and V is the associated certainty equivalent. As Z as the minimum of strictly concave functions is strictly concave, the maximum of Z, therefore, the decision optimal with respect to the $MaxE_{min}$-criterion, is uniquely determined.

---

1) Z is continuous (see (175)).

The optimizations on the left side of (34) can easily be performed. Let (see (10),(12))

$$y^*(\mu,\Omega) = \frac{1}{\alpha}\,\Omega^{-1}(\mu - (1+r)v) \quad ,$$

then it holds (φ is identified with the associated parameters (μ,Ω)):

$$(35) \qquad V = \min_{\varphi\in\Phi}\ \max_{y\in\mathbb{R}^n} \upsilon_\varphi(g(X,y))$$

$$= \min_{(\mu,\Omega)\in\Theta} \upsilon_\varphi(g(X,y^*(\mu,\Omega)))$$

$$= \min_{(\mu,\Omega)\in\Theta} [w(1+r) + \frac{1}{2\alpha}(\mu - (1+r)v)^T\,\Omega^{-1}\,(\mu - (1+r)v)]$$

$$= w(1+r) + \frac{1}{2\alpha}(\tilde{\tilde{\mu}}^* - (1+r)v)^T\,\tilde{\tilde{\Omega}}^{*-1}\,(\tilde{\tilde{\mu}}^* - (1+r)v)$$

and it is shown that (28) specifies the certainty equivalent of an optimal decision.

According to (34), $\upsilon_\varphi(g(X,y))$ has an equilibrium point (y^*,φ^*) (see for example Burger [1966], p. 58):

$$(36) \qquad \upsilon_{\varphi^*}(g(X,y)) \le V = \upsilon_{\varphi^*}(g(X,y^*)) \le \upsilon_\varphi(g(X,y^*)) \quad \forall\varphi\in\Phi \quad \forall y\in\mathbb{R}^n$$

According to (35), especially $\tilde{\tilde{\varphi}}^*$ - the density of an $N(\tilde{\tilde{\mu}}^*,\tilde{\tilde{\Omega}}^*)$-distribution - is an equilibrium strategy:

$$\max_{y\in\mathbb{R}^n} \upsilon_{\tilde{\tilde{\varphi}}^*}(g(X,y)) = V \ .$$

For an equilibrium strategy y^*, (36) yields $(\varphi^* = \tilde{\tilde{\varphi}}^*)$:

$$(37) \qquad \max_{y\in\mathbb{R}^n} \upsilon_{\tilde{\tilde{\varphi}}^*}(g(X,y)) = \upsilon_{\tilde{\tilde{\varphi}}^*}(g(X,y^*)) \ .$$

As $\tilde{\tilde{\Omega}}^*$ is positive definite, the maximum in (37) is uniquely determined (see (27)):

$$y^* = y^*(\tilde{\tilde{\mu}}^*,\tilde{\tilde{\Omega}}^*) = \tilde{\tilde{y}}^* \ .$$

$(\tilde{\tilde{y}}^*,\tilde{\tilde{\varphi}}^*)$ is, therefore, an equilibrium point. (34),(36) result in:

$$\min_{\varphi\in\Phi} \upsilon_\varphi(g(X,\tilde{\tilde{y}}^*)) = V = \max_{y\in\mathbb{R}^n}\ \min_{\varphi\in\Phi} \upsilon_\varphi(g(X,y)) \ ,$$

i.e. $\tilde{\tilde{y}}^* = y^*(\tilde{\tilde{\mu}}^*,\tilde{\tilde{\Omega}}^*)$ is an optimal portfolio decision.

If $((1+r)v,\Omega)\in\Theta$ for one Ω, $\tilde{\tilde{y}}^* = 0$ is obviously true, i.e. the whole initial wealth is invested without risk. Here, the pessimism shows which is characteristic for the MaxE_{min}-principle, similarly as for the Minimax-principle.

As the convex combination of positive definite matrices is again positive definite, the demand of convexity of Θ can not only be fulfilled in special cases - as for example knowing the covariance matrix.

Example 1:

Let $\Omega_1,\ldots,\Omega_k \in \mathbb{R}^{(n,n)}$ be positive definite matrices, $\{\Omega_1,\ldots,\Omega_k\}^K$ the convex closure of $\{\Omega_1,\ldots,\Omega_k\}$, and $\Theta_1 \subset \mathbb{R}^n$ compact and convex (for example an n-dimensional interval), then

$$\Theta := \Theta_1 \times \{\Omega_1,\ldots,\Omega_k\}^K$$

is compact and convex and, hence fulfills the presumption of theorem 2 (see (165)).

Example 2:

Let $\underline{\mu},\bar{\mu} \in \mathbb{R}^n$, $\underline{\Omega}$, $\bar{\Omega} \in \mathbb{R}^{(n,n)}$ be positive definite and (componentwise) $\underline{\mu} \le \bar{\mu}$, $\underline{\Omega} \le \bar{\Omega}$. The following sets are considered:

$$\Theta_1 := [\underline{\mu},\bar{\mu}] := \{\mu \in \mathbb{R}^n : \underline{\mu} \le \mu \le \bar{\mu}\}$$
$$\Theta_2 := \{\Omega : \underline{\Omega} \le \Omega \le \bar{\Omega} \text{ and } \Omega \text{ positive definite}\}$$
$$\Theta := \Theta_1 \times \Theta_2$$

Θ_1 is non-empty, compact and convex. Θ_2 is non-empty, bounded and convex, because:

- $\underline{\Omega},\bar{\Omega} \in \Theta_2$
- $\Omega_1,\Omega_2 \in \Theta_2, \lambda \in [0,1] \Rightarrow$
  $\Omega = \lambda\Omega_1 + (1-\lambda)\Omega_2$ is positive definite (see (165)) and $\underline{\Omega} \le \Omega \le \bar{\Omega}$.

The boundedness of Θ_2 is evident, however, Θ_2 does not have to be compact. The limit of positive definite matrices is generally only positive semidefinite. Thus for the positive definite matrices

$$\underline{\Omega} = \begin{pmatrix} 1 & 0 \\ 0 & 1 \end{pmatrix} \quad , \quad \bar{\Omega} = \begin{pmatrix} 2 & 1 \\ 1 & 2 \end{pmatrix}$$

in fact, $\Omega = \begin{pmatrix} 1 & \beta \\ \beta & 1 \end{pmatrix} \in \Theta_2$ for each $\beta \in [0,1)$, but $\begin{pmatrix} 1 & 1 \\ 1 & 1 \end{pmatrix} \notin \Theta_2$.

Obviously, however, for this example the following is true:

(38) Θ_2 is compact $\Leftrightarrow \exists\, \varepsilon > 0 : \forall\, \Omega \in \Theta_2 : |\Omega| \ge \varepsilon$

However, usually and, in particular, for big n this condition is hard to verify.

If θ_2 is compact, then θ is compact and convex, and $\tilde{\tilde{y}}^*$ can be determined according to theorem 2.

(38) allows an interesting interpretation of this example, and in fact in the sense how precisely an investor should numerically determine his prior data (μ,Ω) , and how these inaccuracies take effect on the decision-making. As the determinant is a continuous function, a $\delta > 0$ - however dependent on Ω - can be found such that a determination of Ω with a componentwise precision of $\pm\delta$ guarantees the validity of the second condition of (38). By this, the presumptions of theorem 2 are fulfilled - independent of how precisely μ is determined. The investor should determine the least favourable prior distribution $(\tilde{\tilde{\mu}}^*,\tilde{\tilde{\Omega}}^*)$ according to (29) within his range of precision and realize the corresponding optimal portfolio $\tilde{\tilde{y}}^*$.[1]

2.3 Information Systems

The hybrid model described in Sec. 2.1 and the modifications presented in Sec. 2.2, respectively allow solving the portfolio probelm, if the prior information level is fixed.[2] Now it is examined how the information level of the investor changes with increasing information. In Sec. 2.4, the value of such an information activity is analyzed.

The term *information system* is used in the statistical sense, i.e. an information system is a t-dimensional random variable Z , whose distribution is described by the likelihood-densities $f_x(z)\,(x \in \mathbb{R}^n\,,\, z \in \mathbb{R}^t)$.[3] By this, the statistic connection between the *message* z and the end-of-period prices are presented. If no relation exists between z and x or if this one is not - at least approximatively - known, then an information processing and evaluation in the pragmatic sense is not possible.

---

[1] If the investor accepts the $\mathrm{MaxE_{min}}$-principle. The optimal portfolio of course depends on the chosen precision. By (38) only a certain minimum-precision is prescribed for Ω .

[2] or - according to Sec. 2.2 - for fixed incomplete prior knowledge.

[3] Only continuous random variables are considered.

If at all, the investor will observe the information system before his portfolio decision, therefore at the beginning of the period. A later information activity is insignificant for the decision-making, and, hence is not considered. The realization of Z before X has the consequence that, realistically no deterministic connection can be assumed. Therefore, Z usually is not complete, i.e. it cannot surely be concluded to x from z .

However, the investor does not have to observe the information system. He stands before the *information decision* whether he decides without further information because of his prior information level, or whether he observes the information system Z where costs independent of the special realization arise, and whether he then decides because of the information level improved by this. The information decision is made by comparing the information cost with the information value - determined in Sec. 2.4 - which specifies the maximum tolerable information cost. The information value is determined comparing the investment results of the optimal decisions at the end of the period with or without information. A direct comparison with the information cost is, therefore, only possible, if this cost is also referred to the end of the period, i.e. if it is discounted. It is characteristic that the information decision has to be made before knowing the realization z . Correspondingly, it is only meaningful to evaluate a whole information system and not a single message.

If the prior knowledge of the investor can be described by a prior density $\varphi(x)$, then his information level after accessing the message z is characterized corresponding to the Bayes formula by the *posterior density* (39)

(39) $$\varphi_z(x) = \frac{f_x(z)\ \varphi(x)}{f(z)}$$

where

(40) $$f(z) = \int f_x(z)\varphi(x)dx$$

is the marginal (unconditional) density of Z . After having accessed the information z , the investor, therefore, replaces his prior density φ by φ_z and determines his optimal portfolio using (9).[1)]

---

1) This corresponds to the hybrid model (Sec. 2.1), but also the modifications 2.2.1,2.2.2 finally lead to a single prior distribution, see (15),(23). The situation 2.2.3 is different: Here - analogous to the Minimax-principle - it is necessary to consider strategies (decision functions), see Sec. 2.4.4 .

However, it has to be assumed for this that the hybrid model is not left by the information activity. Therefore, in the following, only information systems are considered which assuming a prior normal distribution always lead to posterior normally distributed prices. The following theorem describes a big class of such information systems:

Theorem 3:

Given are $\mu \in \mathbb{R}^n$, positive definite matrices $\Omega \in \mathbb{R}^{(n,n)}$, $\Sigma \in \mathbb{R}^{(t,t)}$, and a matrix $T \in \mathbb{R}^{(t,n)}$ with $\operatorname{rank}(T) = t$. Let X be prior $N(\mu,\Omega)$-distributed:

$$X \sim N(\mu,\Omega) \ ,$$

and let the information system Z be an unbiased, normally distributed estimator for Tx with covariance matrix Σ :

$$(41) \qquad Z\big|_{X=x} \sim N(Tx,\Sigma) \qquad \forall\, x \in \mathbb{R}^n$$

then the following is true:

$$(42) \qquad X\big|_{Z=z} \sim N((T^T\Sigma^{-1}T+\Omega^{-1})^{-1}(T^T\Sigma^{-1}z+\Omega^{-1}\mu),\,(T^T\Sigma^{-1}T+\Omega^{-1})^{-1}) \qquad \forall\, z \in \mathbb{R}^t$$

$$(43) \qquad Z \sim N(T\mu,\, T\,\Omega\, T^T + \Sigma)$$

The theorem is the generalization of a standard statement about conjugated prior distributions as it is found, e.g. at LaValle [1970].[1] (41) describes the likelihood-desity, (42) the posterior distribution and (43) the marginal distribution of Z .

The assumption rank(T)=t implies $t \leq n$ and does not present a real limitation, because one can otherwise confine without loss of information to a maximum system of linear independent estimators, i.e. rows of T .

Formally, an information system as described in theorem 3 could be realized by observing the linear transformed, true end-of-period prices, disturbed by an additive error in form of a white noise S , independent of X :

$$Z = TX + S \ , \quad S \sim N(0,\Sigma)$$

However, because of the above addressed, chronological sequence this interpretation has not practical significance.

---

1) for the case that T is the identity matrix.

If Z is an information system according to theorem 3 and $\mathfrak{f}$ an injective, measurable mapping of the $(\mathbb{R}^t, \mathcal{B}^t)$ into a measurable space, then the observarion of $\mathfrak{f}(Z)$ leads to the same posterior distributions (42), to the same posterior optimal portfolio decisions and to the same information value. By theorem 3, therefore, also all information systems are included which supply results that allow a normally distributed, unbiased estimation of any linear transformation of the end-of-period prices. In this sense, it can be imagined that, e.g., accounting information can be included by theorem 3 - at least approximatively.

The following special cases for T show that various real forecast systems can approximatively be described by theorem 3:

- $t = n$: Then, T is nonsingular and all end-of-period prices are simultaneously estimated after a linear transformation of the result by T^{-1} . Because of the big number of risky assets such an information system is practically hardly to realize.

- $T = (t_{ij}) \in \mathbb{R}^{(t,n)}$ with $t_{ij} := \delta(n_i, j)$: [1]The prices of the t assets $n_1, \ldots, n_t$ are simultaneously estimated. Hence, an arbitrarily given subset of assets can be analyzed. In particular, the case of an estimation of a single price is also included.

- $t = 1$: T then is a row vector. If the components of T are the weights of an index, the development of this index is estimated. In the same way, the development of the value of an individual portfolio or - with the aid of negative components - the effect of a portfolio revision can be forecasted.

<u>Proof of theorem 3:</u>

For the numerator of (39), the following is true[2]

$$f_x(z)\varphi(x) = (2\pi)^{-(n+t)/2}|\Omega|^{-1/2}|\Sigma|^{-1/2}e^{-s/2}$$

with

---

[1] δ is the Kronecker-delta: $\delta(i,i) = 1$, $\delta(i,j) = 0$ for $i \neq j$.

[2] '| |' denotes the determinant of a matrix.

$$s = (z - Tx)^T \Sigma^{-1} (z - Tx) + (\mu - x)^T \Omega^{-1} (\mu - x) \quad .$$

As $t = \text{rank}(T) = \text{rank}(TT^T)$ and $TT^T \in \mathbb{R}^{(t,t)}$, TT^T is invertible. Further $T^T\Sigma^{-1}T$ is positive semidefinite and thus $T^T\Sigma^{-1}T + \Omega^{-1}$ positive definite. It follows (see (162))

$$\begin{aligned} s &= (T^T(TT^T)^{-1}z-x)^T T^T \Sigma^{-1} T (T^T(TT^T)^{-1}z-x) + (\mu-x)^T \Omega^{-1} (\mu-x) \\ &= ((T^T\Sigma^{-1}T + \Omega^{-1})^{-1}(T^T\Sigma^{-1}z + \Omega^{-1}\mu)-x)^T (T^T\Sigma^{-1}T + \Omega^{-1}) \\ &\quad ((T^T\Sigma^{-1}T + \Omega^{-1})^{-1}(T^T\Sigma^{-1}z + \Omega^{-1}\mu)-x) \\ &+ (T^T(TT^T)^{-1}z-\mu)^T \Omega^{-1} (T^T\Sigma^{-1}T + \Omega^{-1})^{-1} T^T\Sigma^{-1}T (T^T(TT^T)^{-1}z-\mu) \end{aligned}$$

Hence (42) is true and for $f(z)$ the representation (see (40))

$$f(z) = k \cdot e^{-s'/2} \quad ,$$

follows where k is a constant independent of z and

$$s' = (T^T(TT^T)^{-1}z-\mu)^T \Omega^{-1} (T^T\Sigma^{-1}T + \Omega^{-1})^{-1} T^T\Sigma^{-1}T (T^T(TT^T)^{-1}z-\mu) \quad .$$

It holds (see (167)):

$$\Omega^{-1} (T^T\Sigma^{-1}T + \Omega^{-1})^{-1} T^T\Sigma^{-1}T = T^T (T \Omega T^T + \Sigma)^{-1} T$$

and thus

$$s' = (z - T\mu)^T (T \Omega T^T + \Sigma)^{-1} (z - T\mu) \quad ,$$

i.e. (43). □

The starting-point of theorem 3 corresponds to the hybrid model introduced in Sec. 2.1, but theorem 3 can also be applied for the extensions of the hybrid model introduced in Sec. 2.2.1, Sec. 2.2.2 . If - as in theorem 3 - μ is assumed to be uncertain, it is obvious to consider estimators for $T\mu$ as information systems. The following information system was examined by Kalymon [1971], but only for the case that T is the identity matrix and without considering the information value (see Sec. 2.4.3).

Theorem 4:

Given are $m \in \mathbb{R}^n$, positive definite matrices $\Pi, \Omega \in \mathbb{R}^{(n,n)}$, $\Sigma \in \mathbb{R}^{(t,t)}$ and a matrix $T \in \mathbb{R}^{(t,n)}$ with $\text{rank}(T) = t$. Let M be an $N(m,\Pi)$-distributed random variable:

$$M \sim N(m,\Pi) \quad ,$$

under the condition $'M = \mu'$ let X be $N(\mu,\Omega)$-distributed:

$$X|_{M=\mu} \sim N(\mu,\Omega) \qquad \forall\, \mu \in \mathbb{R}^n \ ,$$

and let Z be an unbiased, normally distributed estimator for $T\mu$ with covariance matrix Σ :

(44) $$Z|_{M=\mu,X=x} \sim N(T\mu,\Sigma) \quad \forall\, \mu\,,\ x \in \mathbb{R}^n \ ,$$

then it holds

(45) $$X|_{Z=z} \sim N((T^T\Sigma^{-1}T + \Pi^{-1})^{-1}(T^T\Sigma^{-1}z + \Pi^{-1}m),\Omega + (T^T\Sigma^{-1}T + \Pi^{-1})^{-1}) \quad \forall\, z \in \mathbb{R}^t$$

(46) $$Z \sim N(Tm, T\,\Pi\, T^T + \Sigma)$$

Hence, also this information system always leads to a normal distribution as posterior distribution. The extended hybrid model is not left by the information activity.

The conditional distribution of Z given in (44) is assumed to be independent of x . This is equivalent to that Z and X are independent under the condition '$M = \mu$' (see the following proof). If μ were known, Z would not be informative for the portfolio problem and, therefore, would be worthless. The information system Z obtains its value by supplying information about μ and, hence also - but only indirectly - about x (see Sec. 2.4.3).

Proof:

According to (15) $X \sim N(m,\Omega + \Pi)$. The density of M is denoted by g . The density of Z dependent on '$M = \mu$' and '$X = x$' is a function h independent of x :

$$f_{\mu,x}(z) = h(\mu,z)$$

$$\Rightarrow f_{\mu}(z) = \frac{1}{g(\mu)} \int h(\mu,z) g_x(\mu) \varphi(x)\, dx$$

$$= h(\mu,z) = f_{\mu,x}(z)$$

$$\Rightarrow Z|_{M=\mu} \sim N(T\mu,\Sigma)$$ [1]

Hence, the situation of theorem 3 is reached, and (46) follows in analogy to (43). The statement corresponding to (42) is:

$$M|_{Z=z} \sim N((T^T\Sigma^{-1}T + \Pi^{-1})^{-1}(T^T\Sigma^{-1}z + \Pi^{-1}m),(T^T\Sigma^{-1}T + \Pi^{-1})^{-1}) \ .$$

Further,

---

1) However, this statement is weaker than (44).

$$\varphi_{z,\mu}(x) = f_{\mu,x}(z) \frac{\varphi_\mu(x)}{f_\mu(z)} = \varphi_\mu(x) \quad , \text{ i.e.}$$

$$X|_{Z=z,M=\mu} \sim N(\mu,\Omega) \quad ,$$

where (45) because of

$$\varphi_z(x) = \int \varphi_{z,\mu}(x)\, g_z(\mu)d\mu$$
$$= \int \varphi_\mu(x) \quad g_z(\mu)d\mu$$

presents a standard statement about conjugate prior distributions (see theorem 1).

Finally, it is shown that the independence of Z and X under the contition '$M = \mu$' is equivalent to the independence of the distribution of $Z|_{M=\mu,X=x}$ of x : Let the common density of Z and X be denoted by h . It holds

$$h_\mu(z,x) = f_{\mu,x}(z)\varphi_\mu(x)$$

and thus

$$f_{\mu,x}(z) = f_\mu(z) \Leftrightarrow h_\mu(z,x) = f_\mu(z)\varphi_\mu(x) \quad .$$ □

2.4 Information Evaluation

The influence of information on the portfolio decision and their value is analyzed for the hybrid model or the extensions considered in Sec. 2.2, respectively. For the information systems introduced in theorem 3 or theorem 4 formulas result which are numerically easy to handle. Some of the following results are taken from Firchau [1984].

2.4.1 The Expected Value of Information and the Amount of Information in the Hybrid Model

It is assumed that the investor defines his pre-knowledge by a prior density φ .[1] Further, let an information system Z be given. Let as well the prior as the posterior distributions (see (39)) be normal distributions.

Independent of defining the *expected value of information* by the selling value EVI_s :

$$\max_y E_\varphi u(g(X,y) + EVI_s) = E_f(\max_y E_{\varphi_Z} u(g(X,y)))$$

---

[1] see Sec. 2.1 or Sec. 2.2.1,2.2.2

or as buying value EVI_b :

(47) $$\max_y E_\varphi u(g(X,y)) = E_f(\max_y E_{\varphi_Z} u(g(X,y) - EVI_b))$$

the same value (see Bamberg, Spremann [1981]):

(48) $$EVI_s = EVI_b = u^{-1}(E_f(\max_y E_{\varphi_Z} u(g(X,y)))) - u^{-1}(\max_y E_\varphi u(g(X,y))) =: EVI$$

results. (47) corresponds to the usual interpretation of the EVI: If costs c ,[1] arise procuring information then

- it is renounced on procuring the information, if $c > EVI$,
- the information is procured, if $c < EVI$,
- the investor is indifferent to the two information alternatives, if $c = EVI$.

Hereby, the portfolio - corresponding to the hybrid model - is evaluated by the expectated utility of the end-of-period wealth determined with regard to the current information level. From (4),(48), it follows immediately:

(49) $$EVI = u^{-1}(E_f u(\max_y \nu_{\varphi_Z}(g(X,y)))) - \max_y \nu_\varphi(g(X,y))$$

As φ and φ_Z are densities of normal distributions,[2] according to (11):

(50) $$EVI = -\frac{1}{\alpha}\ell n\left\{E_f \exp\left[-\frac{1}{2}\left(E_{\varphi_Z}X - (1+r)v\right)^T\left(Cov_{\varphi_Z}X\right)^{-1}\left(E_{\varphi_Z}X - (1+r)v\right)\right]\right\} - \frac{1}{\alpha}\frac{1}{2}(E_\varphi X - (1+r)v)^T(Cov_\varphi X)^{-1}(E_\varphi X - (1+r)v)$$

(50) represents a formula for the EVI for the portfolio problem which can easily be evaluated, if X is as well prior as posterior normally distributed.[3] No presumptions about the marginal distribution - described by f - are necessary. However, it has to be sure that the corresponding functions (see (50)) can be integrated. This is the case for the information systems considered in theorem 3 and theorem 4 (see Sec. 2.4.2,2.4.3).

---

[1] payable at the end of the period.

[2] the assumption of normal distribution is required only now.

[3] Not even an explicit representation of the EVI is possible for any utility function, but for linear and exponential ones, see LaValle [1968], Wenzel [1975].

According to (50), the EVI - as the optimal portfolio decision - is independent of the initial wealth of the investor. This result is a consequence of the consistence axiom and is, correspondingly, not valid for other utility functions; see Wahl [1983].

In the special cases dealt with in the following, a close connection results between the EVI and the amount of information known from the information theory.

For a continuous distribution - described by a density ψ the *entropy* is given by:

$$H(\psi) := -\int \psi(x)\, \ln \psi(x)\, dx$$

The *amount of information* for an information system Z is defined as the difference of the prior entropy and the expected posterior entropy:

(51) $$H(\varphi,Z) := H(\varphi) - E_f\, H(\varphi_Z)$$

If ψ is the density of a normal distribution, then (see Shannon, Weaver [1949])

$$H(\psi) = \ln\left[(2\pi e)^{n/2} |\mathrm{Cov}_\psi X|^{1/2} \right] ,$$

i.e. under the assumption made here, the following is true:

(52) $$H(\varphi,Z) = \frac{1}{2}\, (\ln|\mathrm{Cov}_\varphi X| - E_f\, \ln|\mathrm{Cov}_{\varphi_Z} X|) .$$

A comparison of (48) and (51) shows that the amount of information in opposition to the expected value of information is independent of the underlying result function. Therefore, close connections between these two evaluation concepts can only be expected in special cases. For the information systems defined in Sec. 2.3, it shows in the following that the EVI (see (50)) and $H(\varphi,Z)$ (see (52)) are proportional with α as factor of proportionality.

2.4.2 Unbiased, Normally Distributed Estimators in the Hybrid Model

For the case of a prior normal distribution and for the information systems described in theorem 3, the prior and posterior optimal portfolios, the expected value of information and the amount of information can easily be determined with the aid of the following theorem.

Theorem 5:

Let the assumptions of theorem 3 be fulfilled:

$$X \sim N(\mu, \Omega)$$

$$Z|_{X=x} \sim N(Tx, \Sigma) \quad \forall\, x \in \mathbb{R}^n$$

then the optimal portfolios are prior

(53) $$y^* = \frac{1}{\alpha}\, \Omega^{-1} (\mu - (1+r) v)$$

and posterior, i.e. after having observed z :

(54) $$y^*(z) = y^* + \frac{1}{\alpha} T^T \Sigma^{-1} (z - (1+r) Tv)$$

and the following is true

(55) $$EVI = \frac{1}{2\alpha}\, \ln \frac{|T\Omega T^T + \Sigma|}{|\Sigma|} > 0$$

(56) $$H(\varphi, Z) = \alpha\ EVI$$

Proof:

(53) is equivalent to (10), and (54) immediately follows from (9), (42):

$$y^*(z) = \frac{1}{\alpha}\, [T^T\Sigma^{-1} z + \Omega^{-1}\mu - (1+r)(T^T\Sigma^{-1}T + \Omega^{-1}) v]$$

Next (55) is shown. According to (42),(50), the following is true:

$$EVI = -\frac{1}{\alpha} \ln E_f\, e^{-s''/2}$$

with

$$\begin{aligned} s'' &= ((T^T\Sigma^{-1}T+\Omega^{-1})^{-1}(T^T\Sigma^{-1}z+\Omega^{-1}\mu) - (1+r)v)^T (T^T\Sigma^{-1}T+\Omega^{-1}) \\ &\quad ((T^T\Sigma^{-1}T+\Omega^{-1})^{-1}(T^T\Sigma^{-1}z+\Omega^{-1}\mu) - (1+r)v) \\ &\quad - (\mu - (1+r)v)^T \Omega^{-1} (\mu - (1+r)v) \\ &= (T^T(TT^T)^{-1}z - (1+r)v)^T T^T\Sigma^{-1}T(T^T(TT^T)^{-1}z - (1+r)v) \\ &\quad - (T^T(TT^T)^{-1}z - \mu)^T \Omega^{-1}(T^T\Sigma^{-1}T+\Omega^{-1})^{-1}T^T\Sigma^{-1}T(T^T(TT^T)^{-1}z - \mu) \\ &= (z - (1+r)Tv)^T\Sigma^{-1}(z - (1+r)Tv) - (z - T\mu)^T (T\Omega T^T+\Sigma)^{-1}(z - T\mu) \end{aligned}$$

(see (162),(167)).

With (43), it follows

$$\begin{aligned} E_f\, e^{-s''/2} &= (2\pi)^{-t/2} |T\Omega T^T+\Sigma|^{-1/2} \int \exp\left\{-\frac{1}{2}(z-(1+r)Tv)^T\Sigma^{-1}(z-(1+r)Tv)\right\} dz \\ &= |T\Omega T^T+\Sigma|^{-1/2}\ |\Sigma|^{1/2} \end{aligned}$$

i.e. the equality in (55). The positivity of the EVI immediately follows from (170).

Finally, (56) is shown. According to (42),(52),(168), the following is true:

$$\begin{aligned} H(\varphi,Y) &= \frac{1}{2}(\ell n|\Omega| + E_f\, \ell n|T^T\Sigma^{-1}T+\Omega^{-1}|) \\ &= \frac{1}{2}\,\ell n|\Omega\, T^T\Sigma^{-1}T + Id_n| \\ &= \frac{1}{2}\,\ell n|T\Omega T^T\Sigma^{-1} + Id_t| \\ &= \frac{1}{2}\,\ell n\,\frac{|T\Omega T^T+\Sigma|}{|\Sigma|} \end{aligned}$$

□

The positivity of the EVI (55) and the proportionality (56) are in agreement with the results derived for the logarithmic utility function by Wahl [1983].

According to (54), the portfolio-revision to be done after having obtained the information z is independent of the prior data (μ,Ω):

$$y^*(z) - y^* = \frac{1}{\alpha}T^T\Sigma^{-1}(z - (1+r)Tv)$$

If the investor keeps his prior optimal portfolio before accessing information, then by this the totally resulting acivity of the investor dependent on the information is described. This one can relatively easy be determined.

According to (43), the expected portfolio revisions are

$$E_f[y^*(Z) - y^*] = \frac{1}{\alpha}T^T\Sigma^{-1}\,T(\mu - (1+r)v)$$

If $\mu = (1+r)v$, i.e. if the prior expected rates of return of the risky assets are equal to the risk free rate of return, $y^*=0$ and on average no portfolio revisions occur.

If $U \in \mathbb{R}^{(u,t)}$, $\mathrm{rank}(Z) = u$, then with Z also UZ fulfills the presumptions of theorem 3 or 5:

$$UZ|_{X=x} \sim N(UTx, U\Sigma U^T)$$

The information value of UZ , of course, cannot be greater than the one of Z :

(57) $$EVI(Z) \geq EVI(UZ)$$

where the equality only holds, if $t = u$ (see (170)). Decreasing the number of estimated values, therefore, always leads to a loss of information.

If $\Omega' \succ \Omega$,[1] then it results from (55) with transition from Ω to Ω' and otherwise unchanged data:

(58) $\quad EVI(\Omega') > EVI(\Omega)$

i.e. increasing the prior uncertainty leads to an increasing of the information value (see (169) and Sec. 2.4.3).

According to (55), the expected value of information is independent of μ. This result is a consequence of admitting short sales.

Further (55) shows that the expected value of information is proportional to the inverse risk aversion, i.e. with increasing risk aversion of the investor, the information value decreases. This perhaps at first surprising result can be explained by (53),(54). The entirely riskily invested (or raised) amount $|\sum_{i=1}^{n} y_i^*|$ decreases prior as posterior with increasing risk aversion with the same extent as the EVI. In the extreme case of an infinitely high risk aversion, the investor always invests his whole wealth risk free and, correspondingly, is not interested in any information about the risky assets.

According to (55) $EVI \to \infty$, if $\Sigma \to 0$. The perfect knowledge of Tx has an infinitely high information value, although from this knowledge the true end-of-period prices can only be computed, if $t = n$. Therefore, generally, this is not a perfect information system. This result is only theoretically interesting. In reality, such perfect estimators do not exist. For the practice, a limitation of the information value moreover results from the fact that according to (54), the portfolio revision effected by the information procurement becomes more and more extensive with increasing estimation precision which leads to price changes. The assumption that the information activity does not influence the prices, can then no longer be maintained (regarding this see Sec. 3.3, especially (160)).
In special cases, the determinants in (55) can easily be determined.

Example 3:

If $T\Omega T^T$ and Σ are proportional:

---

1) i.e. $\Omega' - \Omega$ is positive definite.

(59) $\quad T\Omega T^T = a\Sigma \quad a > 0$

then according to (55),

$$EVI = \frac{t}{2\alpha} \ln (1 + a)$$

With increasing a, i.e. with increasing forecast precision EVI increases.

If $\alpha \cdot w = 1$ which is not unrealistic,[1] then

$$EVI = t \cdot w \cdot \ln \sqrt{1+a} \, .$$

For e.g. $a = 0.1$ it results that it can rationally be justified to spend up to 4.8 % of the initial wealth per forecasted value for such an information system.

<u>Example 4:</u>

Assume that $t = 1$, i.e. only one value is forecasted. Then, (59) is always fulfilled. If the $(1,n)$ matrix T is the i-th unit (row) vector e_i^T, then the end-of-period price of the i-th asset is estimated and:[2]

$$EVI = \frac{1}{2\alpha} \ln \left(1 + \frac{\sigma^2}{\omega_i^2}\right)$$

$$y^*(z) - y^* = \frac{z - (1+r)v_i}{\alpha\, \sigma^2} e_i$$

Only revisions with regard to the i-th asset - as expected - take place:

$$y_i^*(z) = y_i^* + \frac{z - (1+r)v_i}{\alpha\, \sigma^2}$$

$$y_j^*(z) = y_j^* \quad \text{for} \quad j \neq i \, .$$

---

1) see Bamberg, Spremann [1981].

2) ω_i^2 is the prior variance of the i-th asset and σ^2 the estimation variance.

2.4.3 Unbiased, Normally Distributed Estimators if a Risk Situation with Regard to the Prior Parameters is Assumed

In Sec. 2.2.1 and 2.2.2, two extension possibilities of the hybrid model were examined for the case that regarding the prior parameters - especially μ - a risk situation is assumed. It showed that in both cases the problem can be reduced to the hybrid model approach (see (15),(23)). For the information systems presented in theorem 3 the expected value of information is, therefore, determined analogously to theorem 5. While for Lin's approach (Sec. 2.2.2) according to (23) exactly the results (53) to (56) of theorem 5 follow,[1] the expected value of information increases if the two-level Bayes approach (Sec. 2.2.1) is assumed.

Theorem 6:

Let the assumptions of theorem 1 be fulfilled:

$$M \sim N(m, \Pi)$$

$$X|_{M=\mu} \sim N(\mu, \Omega) \quad \forall\ \mu \in \mathbb{R}^n$$

then for the information system Z considered in theorem 3

$$Z|_{X=x} \sim N(Tx, \Sigma) \quad \forall\ x \in \mathbb{R}^n$$

the following results follow:

(60) $$\tilde{y}^* = \frac{1}{\alpha}\ (\Omega+\Pi)^{-1}(m - (1+r)v)$$

is the prior and

(61) $$\tilde{y}^*(z) = \tilde{y}^* + \frac{1}{\alpha} T^T \Sigma^{-1}(z - (1+r)Tv)$$

the posterior optimal portfolio after having observed z, and it holds:

(62) $$EVI = \frac{1}{2\alpha}\ \ell n\ \frac{|T(\Omega+\Pi)T^T + \Sigma|}{|\Sigma|} > 0$$

(63) $$H(\tilde{\varphi}, Z) = \alpha\ EVI$$

Thereby, $\tilde{\varphi}$ is the prior density of X resulting from the two-level approach and described in (15).

---

[1] where in (53) μ has to be replaced by m.

Proof:

According to theorem 1 $X \sim N(m, \Omega+\Pi)$, and theorem 6 immediately follows from theorem 5, if there μ is replaced by m and Ω by $\Omega + \Pi$. □

The posterior distribution of X and the marginal distribution of Z can be determined analogously to (42),(43).

As Π is positive definite, $\Omega + \Pi > \Omega$ holds and if μ is uncertain, according to (58) a greater expected value of information (62) results than with known prior parameters (55).

As mentioned, it is obvious to consider estimators for $T\mu$ if μ is uncertain. Also for the information systems introduced in theorem 4, the expected value of information can easily be determined.

Theorem 7:

Let the assumption of theorem 4 be fulfilled:

$$M \sim N(m, \Pi)$$

$$X|_{M=\mu} \sim N(\mu, \Omega) \qquad \forall\ \mu \in \mathbb{R}^n$$

$$Z|_{M=\mu, X=x} \sim N(T\mu, \Sigma) \qquad \forall\ \mu, x \in \mathbb{R}^n$$

then

(64) $$\tilde{y}^* = \frac{1}{\alpha}\ (\Omega+\Pi)^{-1}(m - (1+r)v)$$

is the prior and

(65) $$\tilde{y}^*(z) = \frac{1}{\alpha}\ (\Omega+\Pi+\Pi\ T^T\ \Sigma^{-1}\ T\ \Omega)^{-1}(m - (1+\underline{r})v + \Pi\ T^T\ \Sigma^{-1}(z - (1+r)Tv))$$

the posterior optimal portfolio after having observed z , and it holds:

(66) $$EVI = \frac{1}{2\alpha}\ \ln \frac{|T\Pi T^T+\Sigma|}{|T(\Omega^{-1}+\Pi^{-1})^{-1}T^T+\Sigma|} > 0$$

(67) $$H(\tilde{\varphi}, Z) = \alpha\ EVI$$

Thereby, $\tilde{\varphi}$ again is the prior distribution of X resulting from the two-level approach and described in (15).

Proof:

The statement (64) immediately follows from (15) and (65) from (45):

$$\tilde{y}^*(z) = \frac{1}{\alpha}(\Omega+(T^T\Sigma^{-1}T+\Pi^{-1})^{-1})^{-1}((T^T\Sigma^{-1}T+\Pi^{-1})^{-1}(T^T\Sigma^{-1}z+\Pi^{-1}m)-(1+r)v)$$

$$= \frac{1}{\alpha}(T^T\Sigma^{-1}T\Omega+\Pi^{-1}\Omega+Id)^{-1}(\Pi^{-1}(m-(1+r)v)+T^T\Sigma^{-1}(y-(1+r)Tv))$$

Next the equality in (66) is shown. According to (45),(46),(50):

$$EVI = -\frac{1}{\alpha}\ell n\left\{(2\pi)^{-t/2}|T\Pi T^T+\Sigma|^{-1/2}\int e^{-s/2}dz\right\}$$

with (see(167)):

$$\begin{aligned}
s = {} & (Tm-z)^T(T\Pi T^T+\Sigma)^{-1}(Tm-z) \\
& + ((T^T\Sigma^{-1}T+\Pi^{-1})^{-1}(T^T\Sigma^{-1}z+\Pi^{-1}m)-(1+r)v)^T(\Omega+(T^T\Sigma^{-1}T+\Pi^{-1})^{-1})^{-1} \\
& \quad ((T^T\Sigma^{-1}T+\Pi^{-1})^{-1}(T^T\Sigma^{-1}z+\Pi^{-1}m)-(1+r)v)-(m-(1+r)v)^T(\Pi+\Omega)^{-1}(m-(1+r)v) \\
= {} & (T(m-(1+r)v)-(z-(1+r)Tv))^T(\Sigma^{-1}-\Sigma^{-1}T(T^T\Sigma^{-1}T+\Pi^{-1})^{-1}T^T\Sigma^{-1}) \\
& \quad (T(m-(1+r)v)-(z-(1+r)Tv)) \\
& + (\Pi^{-1}(m-(1+r)v)+T^T\Sigma^{-1}(z-(1+r)Tv))^T((T^T\Sigma^{-1}T+\Pi^{-1})^{-1}-(T^T\Sigma^{-1}T+\Pi^{-1}+\Omega^{-1})^{-1}) \\
& \quad (\Pi^{-1}(m-(1+r)v)+T^T\Sigma^{-1}(z-(1+r)Tv))-(m-(1+r)v)^T(\Pi+\Omega)^{-1}(m-(1+r)v) \\
= {} & (z-(1+r)Tv)^T(\Sigma+T(\Pi^{-1}+\Omega^{-1})^{-1}T^T)^{-1}(z-(1+r)Tv) \\
& + (m-(1+r)v)^T\Pi^{-1}(\Pi^{-1}+\Omega^{-1})^{-1}T^T(\Sigma+T(\Pi^{-1}+\Omega^{-1})^{-1}T^T)^{-1}T(\Pi^{-1}+\Omega^{-1})^{-1}\Pi^{-1}(m-(1+r)v) \\
& - 2(z-(1+r)Tv)^T(\Sigma+T(\Pi^{-1}+\Omega^{-1})^{-1}T^T)^{-1}T(\Pi^{-1}+\Omega^{-1})^{-1}\Pi^{-1}(m-(1+r)v) \\
= {} & (z-(1+r)Tv-T(\Pi^{-1}+\Omega^{-1})^{-1}\Pi^{-1}(m-(1+r)v))^T(\Sigma+T(\Pi^{-1}+\Omega^{-1})^{-1}T^T)^{-1} \\
& \quad (z-(1+r)Tv-T(\Pi^{-1}+\Omega^{-1})^{-1}\Pi^{-1}(m-(1+r)v))
\end{aligned}$$

The last but one equation is true because of (see (167)):

$$\begin{aligned}
& \Sigma^{-1}-\Sigma^{-1}T(T^T\Sigma^{-1}T+\Pi^{-1})^{-1}T^T\Sigma^{-1} \\
& + \Sigma^{-1}T((T^T\Sigma^{-1}T+\Pi^{-1})^{-1}-(T^T\Sigma^{-1}T+\Pi^{-1}+\Omega^{-1})^{-1})T^T\Sigma^{-1} \\
& = \Sigma^{-1}-\Sigma^{-1}T(T^T\Sigma^{-1}T+\Pi^{-1}+\Omega^{-1})^{-1}T^T\Sigma^{-1} \\
& = (\Sigma+T(\Pi^{-1}+\Omega^{-1})^{-1}T^T)^{-1}
\end{aligned}$$

and

$$\begin{aligned}
& T^T\Sigma^{-1}T-T^T\Sigma^{-1}T(T^T\Sigma^{-1}T+\Pi^{-1})^{-1}T^T\Sigma^{-1}T \\
& + \Pi^{-1}(T^T\Sigma^{-1}T+\Pi^{-1})^{-1}\Pi^{-1}-\Pi^{-1}(T^T\Sigma^{-1}T+\Pi^{-1}+\Omega^{-1})^{-1}\Pi^{-1}-(\Pi+\Omega)^{-1} \\
& = \Pi^{-1}-(\Pi+\Omega)^{-1}-\Pi^{-1}(T^T\Sigma^{-1}T+\Pi^{-1}+\Omega^{-1})^{-1}\Pi^{-1} \\
& = \Pi^{-1}(\Pi^{-1}+\Omega^{-1})^{-1}\Pi^{-1}-\Pi^{-1}(T^T\Sigma^{-1}T+\Pi^{-1}+\Omega^{-1})^{-1}\Pi^{-1} \\
& = \Pi^{-1}(\Pi^{-1}+\Omega^{-1})^{-1}T^T\Sigma^{-1}T(T^T\Sigma^{-1}T+\Pi^{-1}+\Omega^{-1})^{-1}\Pi^{-1} \\
& = \Pi^{-1}(\Pi^{-1}+\Omega^{-1})^{-1}T^T\Sigma^{-1}T(Id-(T^T\Sigma^{-1}T+\Pi^{-1}+\Omega^{-1})^{-1}T^T\Sigma^{-1}T)(\Pi^{-1}+\Omega^{-1})^{-1}\Pi^{-1}
\end{aligned}$$

$$= \Pi^{-1}(\Pi^{-1}+\Omega^{-1})^{-1}T^T(\Sigma^{-1}-\Sigma^{-1}T(T^T\Sigma^{-1}T+\Pi^{-1}+\Omega^{-1})^{-1}T^T\Sigma^{-1})T(\Pi^{-1}+\Omega^{-1})^{-1}\Pi^{-1}$$

$$= \Pi^{-1}(\Pi^{-1}+\Omega^{-1})^{-1}T^T(\Sigma+T(\Pi^{-1}+\Omega^{-1})^{-1}T^T)^{-1}(\Pi^{-1}+\Omega^{-1})^{-1}\Pi^{-1}$$

and finally

$$(\Sigma^{-1}-\Sigma^{-1}T(T^T\Sigma^{-1}T+\Pi^{-1})^{-1}T^T\Sigma^{-1})T$$

$$- \Sigma^{-1}T((T^T\Sigma^{-1}T+\Pi^{-1})^{-1}-(T^T\Sigma^{-1}T+\Pi^{-1}+\Omega^{-1})^{-1})\Pi^{-1}$$

$$= \Sigma^{-1}T(T^T\Sigma^{-1}T+\Pi^{-1}+\Omega^{-1})^{-1}\Pi^{-1}$$

$$= (\Sigma+T(\Pi^{-1}+\Omega^{-1})^{-1}T^T)^{-1}T(\Pi^{-1}+\Omega^{-1})^{-1}\Pi^{-1}$$

As $\Sigma+T(\Pi^{-1}+\Omega^{-1})^{-1}T^T$ is positive definite, it yields:

$$\text{EVI} = -\frac{1}{\alpha}\ln\left[\,|T\Pi T^T+\Sigma|^{-1/2}|\Sigma+T(\Pi^{-1}+\Omega^{-1})^{-1}T^T|^{1/2}\right]$$

and by this the equality in (66) is shown.

(67) follows because of (see (168)):

$$\text{EVI} = \frac{1}{2\alpha}\ln\frac{|T^T\Sigma^{-1}T+\Pi^{-1}|\,|\Pi|}{|(\Pi^{-1}+\Omega^{-1})^{-1}|\,|T^T\Sigma^{-1}T+\Pi^{-1}+\Omega^{-1}|} = \frac{1}{2\alpha}\ln\frac{|\Pi+\Omega|}{|(T^T\Sigma^{-1}T+\Pi^{-1})^{-1}+\Omega|}$$

from (15),(45),(51). The EVI is positive (see (66)) because

$$\Pi+\Omega-((T^T\Sigma^{-1}T+\Pi^{-1})^{-1}+\Omega) = (T^T\Sigma^{-1}T+\Pi^{-1})^{-1}[T^T\Sigma^{-1}T\Pi T^T\Sigma^{-1}T+T^T\Sigma^{-1}T](T^T\Sigma^{-1}T+\Pi^{-1})^{-1}$$

is positive semidefinite and unequal to the null-matrix (see (169)). □

Under the assumptions about Ω,Π,Σ,T, which underly theorem 6, theorem 7 respectively (see (170)), the following is true:

$$|T(\Omega+\Pi)T^T+\Sigma| > |T\Pi T^T+\Sigma|$$

$$|T(\Omega^{-1}+\Pi^{-1})^{-1}T^T+\Sigma| > |\Sigma|$$

i.e. the expected value of information in the situation of theorem 6 (62) is always greater than the one in the situation of theorem 7 (66). With the same preknowledge and the same precision the estimation of the end-of-period prices is more valuable than the estimation of the expectations of these prices.

2.4.4 Information Evaluation if Partial Uncertainty with Regard to the Prior Parameters is Assumed

Also if other optimality criteria than the Bayes rule are taken as a basis, the value of an information system can be determined in many cases.[1] In particular, this is also possible for the situation described in Sec. 2.2.3, i.e. for the MaxE_{min}-principle which is now assumed.

Let an information system Z be given which fulfills the presuppositions of theorem 3:

$$Z|_{X=x} \sim N(Tx,\Sigma)$$

A pointwise determination of the portfolio decision after information access analogously (54) with the aid of posterior distributions is at first not possible. Rather decision functions:[2]

$$\delta : \mathbb{R}^t \rightarrow \mathbb{R}^n$$

have to be considered. As in Sec. 2.2.3 let Φ be the class of possible prior distributions which only contains normal distributions, and let Θ be the associated range of parameters which fulfills the presuppositions of theorem 2, i.e. which is compact and convex.

Analogously to the EVI, the *Φ-value of the information* (ΦVI) specifies the information cost maximum tolerable by the investor. Corresponding to (47), the ΦVI is implicitly defined as solution of the equation:

$$\max_{y\in\mathbb{R}^n} \min_{\varphi\in\Phi} E_\varphi\, u(g(X,y)) = \sup_{\delta\in\Delta} \inf_{\varphi\in\Phi} E_\varphi\, E_{f_X}\, u(g(X,\delta(Z)) - \Phi VI) \qquad (60)$$

Thereby, Δ is the class of admitted decision functions,[3] which should at least contain all linear functions.[4] Whether the supremum

---

1) See, e.g. Albach [1969], Bamberg [1974,1975], Ferschl [1975], Bamberg, Coenenberg, Kleine-Doepke [1976], Firchau [1980a].

2) A decision $\delta(z)$ is assigned to each possible information z .

3) Not all mappings of the $\mathbb{R}^t$ into the $\mathbb{R}^n$ can be admitted because of measurability reasons.

4) In order to include the Bayes solutions in Δ , see (54). Strictly speaking, this assumption was also based upon in Sec. 2.4.2, 2.4.3 .

in (68) is attained, depends on Δ . Also if no optimal δ^* exists, the ΦVI can be interpreted as an information value: If the information cost is smaller than the ΦVI, then procuring the information pays. Only if they are equal, the indifference is no longer given, but then it should already be renounced on procuring the information.

By (68), the ΦVI is defined as buying value. An analogous definition as selling value is possible, but leads to the same result, namely:[1)]

$$\text{(69)} \qquad \Phi VI = u^{-1}\left[\sup_{\delta \in \Delta} \inf_{\varphi \in \Phi} E_{\varphi} E_{f_X} u(g(X,\delta(Z)))\right] - u^{-1}\left[\max_{y \in \mathbb{R}^n} \min_{\varphi \in \Phi} E_{\varphi} u(g(X,y))\right]$$

Therefore, also in this case one obtains an explicit solution. Theorem 2 immediately yields:

$$\text{(70)} \qquad \Phi VI = \sup_{\delta \in \Delta} \inf_{\varphi \in \Phi} u^{-1}\left[E_f E_{\varphi_Z} u(g(X,\delta(Z)))\right] - \left[w(1+r) + \frac{1}{2\alpha} \min_{(\mu,\Omega) \in \Theta} (\mu - (1+r)v)^T \Omega^{-1} (\mu - (1+r)v)\right]$$

Φ and Δ are fixed, then the ΦVI can be determined with the aid of (70). Besides, from (70) a simple upper bound for the ΦVI results (see (12),(49),(55)):

$$\text{(71)} \qquad \Phi VI \leq \inf_{\varphi \in \Phi} \sup_{\delta \in \Delta} u^{-1}\left[E_f E_{\varphi_Z} u(g(X,\delta(Z)))\right] - \left[w(1+r) + \frac{1}{2\alpha} \min_{(\mu,\Omega) \in \Theta} (\mu - (1+r)v)^T \Omega^{-1} (\mu - (1+r)v)\right]$$

$$= \min_{\varphi \in \Phi} \max_{\delta \in \Delta} u^{-1}(E_f\, u(\nu_{\varphi_Z}(g(X,\delta(Z))))) - \left[w(1+r) + \frac{1}{2\alpha} \min_{(\mu,\Omega) \in \Theta} (\mu - (1+r)v)^T \Omega^{-1} (\mu - (1+r)v)\right]$$

$$= \frac{1}{2\alpha} \min_{(\mu,\Omega) \in \Theta} \left[\ln \frac{|T\Omega T^T + \Sigma|}{|\Sigma|} + (\mu - (1+r)v)^T \Omega^{-1} (\mu - (1+r)v)\right] - \frac{1}{2\alpha} \min_{(\mu,\Omega) \in \Theta} (\mu - (1+r)v)^T \Omega^{-1} (\mu - (1+r)v) .$$

---

1) The proof of (69) is analogous to the proof of (48); again the constancy of the absolute risk aversion is essential.

If 'sup' and 'inf' in (70) can be exchanged, then in (71) the equality sign holds.

The case that only one covariance matrix Ω is thought to be possible is interesting. In this case, 'sup' and 'inf' can be exchanged, and the extrema are attained:

Theorem 8:

Let the presuppositions of theorem 2 be fulfilled, and let Ω be known, i.e. there is a positive definite matrix $\Omega \in \mathbb{R}^{(n,n)}$ and a compact, convex set $\Theta_1 \in \mathbb{R}^n$ with $\Theta = \{(\mu,\Omega) : \mu \in \Theta_1\}$. Then for the information system Z introduced in theorem 3 holds:

There is a $\mathrm{MaxE}_{\min}$-optimal decision function δ^* with:

$$\delta^*(z) = \frac{1}{\alpha}\,\Omega^{-1}(\tilde{\tilde{\mu}}^* - (1+r)v) + \frac{1}{\alpha}T^T\Sigma^{-1}(z - (1+r)Tv) \quad \forall\, z \in \mathbb{R}^t ,$$

where $\tilde{\tilde{\mu}}^*$ is determined according to (29). The corresponding information value yields as:

$$\Phi VI = \frac{1}{2\alpha}\,\ln \frac{|T\Omega T^T + \Sigma|}{|\Sigma|} \tag{72}$$

Ω is fixed, therefore, for the amount of information the same value results for any $\varphi \in \Phi$, namely (see (56)):

$$H(\varphi,Z) = \alpha\ \Phi VI \quad \forall \quad \varphi \in \Phi .$$

$\tilde{\tilde{\mu}}^*$ is with as well as without information the most unfavourable expectation vector.

If $(1+r)v \in \Theta_1$, then $\tilde{\tilde{\mu}}^* = (1+r)v$ and $\delta^*(z) = \frac{1}{\alpha}T^T\Sigma^{-1}(z - (1+r)Tv)$ (see Sec. 2.2.3). While in this case prior the whole initial wealth is invested without any risk, after information access a risky portfolio is built up.

According to (55), the ΦVI is equal to the corresponding EVI. A comparison with theorem 7 shows that uncertainty about μ increases the information value only if a risk situation is assumed, while the corresponding information value remains unchanged if an uncertainty situation is assumed.

Proof:

As Ω is known, according to (71) it must essentially be shown that in (70) 'sup' and 'inf' can be exchanged. Firstly, this is only shown for

$$\bar{\Delta} := \{\delta_y : \delta_y(z) = \frac{1}{\alpha}(y + T^T\Sigma^{-1}z),\ y \in \mathbb{R}^n\}\ .$$

According to (54), $\bar{\Delta}$ is the set of all Bayes solutions. $\bar{\Delta}$ can be identified with the $\mathbb{R}^n$ and is convex and closed.

Let for $y \in \mathbb{R}^n$, $\mu \in \Theta_1$:[1]

$$u^{-1}(E_f\, E_{\varphi_Z}\, u(g(X,\delta_y(Z)))) =: F(\mu,y)$$

According to (173) it suffices to show that $F(\mu,y)$ is convex as a function of μ and concave as a function of y. Let $\bar{y}^* := \Omega^{-1}\mu - (1+r)(T^T\Sigma^{-1}T+\Omega^{-1})v$.

According to (6),(42):

$$\begin{aligned} v_{\varphi_z}(g(X,\delta_y(z))) &= w(1+r) + \frac{1}{\alpha}(y+T^T\Sigma^{-1}z)^T(T^T\Sigma^{-1}T+\Omega^{-1})^{-1} \\ &\quad (T^T\Sigma^{-1}z+\Omega^{-1}\mu - (1+r)(T^T\Sigma^{-1}T+\Omega^{-1})v - \frac{1}{2}(y+T^T\Sigma^{-1}z)) \\ &= w(1+r) + \frac{1}{2\alpha}(y+T^T\Sigma^{-1}z)^T(T^T\Sigma^{-1}T+\Omega^{-1})^{-1}(T^T\Sigma^{-1}z-y+2\bar{y}^*) \\ &= F_1(y) + F_2(z) \end{aligned}$$

with

$$F_1(y) := -\frac{1}{2\alpha}(y-\bar{y}^*)^T(T^T\Sigma^{-1}T+\Omega^{-1})^{-1}(y-\bar{y}^*)$$

$$\begin{aligned} F_2(z) &:= w(1+r) + \frac{1}{2\alpha} z^T\Sigma^{-1}T(T^T\Sigma^{-1}T+\Omega^{-1})^{-1}(T^T\Sigma^{-1}z+2\bar{y}^*) \\ &\quad + \frac{1}{2\alpha}\bar{y}^*(T^T\Sigma^{-1}T+\Omega^{-1})^{-1}\bar{y}^* \end{aligned}$$

As the certainty equivalent can be decomposed, it results corresponding to the consistence condition for exponential utility functions:

$$F(\mu,y) = u^{-1}E_f\, u(F_1(y) + F_2(Z)) = F_1(y) + u^{-1}E_f\, u(F_2(Z))$$

Especially for $y = \bar{y}^*$

$$F(\mu,\bar{y}^*) = \frac{1}{2\alpha}\ln\frac{|T\Omega T^T + \Sigma|}{|\Sigma|} + \frac{1}{2\alpha}(\mu - (1+r)v)^T\Omega^{-1}(\mu - (1+r)v)$$

$$F_1(\bar{y}^*) = 0$$

---

1) φ is the density of an $N(\mu,\Omega)$-distribution.

are true because of $\delta_{\bar{y}^*}(z) = y^*(z)$ (see (49),(55),(55),(71)).
Altogether, it follows for any $y \in \mathbb{R}^n$, $\mu \in \Theta_1$:

$$F(\mu,y) = F_1(y) + F(\mu,\bar{y}^*)$$

$$= \frac{1}{2\alpha}\left[\ell n\,\frac{|T\Omega T^T + \Sigma|}{|\Sigma|} + (\mu - (1+r)v)^T\Omega^{-1}(\mu - (1+r)v)\right.$$

$$- (y - \Omega^{-1}(\mu - (1+r)v) + (1+r)T^T\Sigma^{-1}Tv)^T(T^T\Sigma^{-1}T+\Omega^{-1})^{-1}$$

$$\left.(y - \Omega^{-1}(\mu - (1+r)v) + (1+r)T^T\Sigma^{-1}Tv)\right]$$

As $T^T\Sigma^{-1}T + \Omega^{-1}$ is positive definite and (see (167))

$$\Omega^{-1} - \Omega^{-1}(T^T\Sigma^{-1}T+\Omega^{-1})^{-1}\Omega^{-1}$$

$$= \Omega^{-1}(T^T\Sigma^{-1}T+\Omega^{-1})^{-1}T^T\Sigma^{-1}T$$

$$= T^T(T\Omega T^T+\Sigma)^{-1}T$$

is positive semidefinite, F is convex as a function of μ and concave as a function of y . Thus

$$\sup_{\delta\in\bar{\Delta}}\ \inf_{\varphi\in\Phi} E_\varphi E_{f_X}\ u(g(X,\delta(Z))) = \inf_{\varphi\in\Phi}\ \sup_{\delta\in\bar{\Delta}} E_\varphi E_{f_X}\ u(g(X,\delta(Z)))$$

and (72) follows for $\Delta = \bar{\Delta}$.

As Θ_1 is compact and F continuous, the infima and the one supremum are attained (see (71)):

$$\min_{\varphi\in\Phi}\ \max_{\delta\in\bar{\Delta}} E_\varphi E_{f_X}\ u(g(X,\delta(Z))) = \sup_{\delta\in\bar{\Delta}}\ \min_{\varphi\in\Phi} E_\phi E_{f_X}\ u(g(X,\delta(Z)))$$

Analogously to the proof of theorem 2, it follows that also the last supremum is attained. Hence, there is a most unfavourable prior expectation $\bar{\mu}^*$ and a $\mathrm{MaxE}_{\min}$-optimal decision function δ^* which can be determined according to (53),(54):

$$\delta^*(z) = \frac{1}{\alpha}\,\Omega^{-1}(\bar{\mu}^* - (1+r)v) + \frac{1}{\alpha}T^T\,\Sigma^{-1}(z - (1+r)Tv)$$

where $\bar{\mu}^*$ minimizes the associated certainty equivalent with respect to all possible Bayes solutions:

$$F(\bar{\mu}^*,\bar{y}^*) = \min_{\mu\in\Theta_1}\ \max_{y\in\mathbb{R}^n} F(\mu,y)$$

$$= \min_{\mu\in\Theta_1}\left[\frac{1}{2\alpha}\ell n\frac{|T\Omega T^T + \Sigma|}{|\Sigma|} + \frac{1}{2\alpha}\ (\mu - (1+r)v)^T\Omega^{-1}(\mu - (1+r)v)\right],$$

i.e. $\bar{\mu}^*$ is a solution of (29) for the special case 'Ω known' considered here: $\bar{\mu}^* = \tilde{\tilde{\mu}}^*$.

It follows immediately from (174) that the statements of theorem 8 remain valid also for $\Delta \supset \bar{\Delta}$. □

3. Information Processing and Information Evaluation if Information Effected Changes of the Equilibirum Prices are Considered

In Sec. 2, it was assumed that the prices at the beginning of the period are exogeneously given and not influenced by the information activity. Now the information problems are treated within the framework of a market model. The presupposed equilibrium prices reflect the expectations of the investors and change correspondingly, if the expectations of the market participants are influenced by an information activity. Information activity is here interpreted as the observation of an information system by a defined group of investors where it is presupposed that the other investors do not obtain any additional information, and that their expectations, correspondingly, do not change. Such a consideration, of course, is only possible for a capital market model which allows heterogeneous expectations. For even if prior all investors have homogeneous expectations, the information activity usually[1] leads to posterior inhomogeneous expectations. In Sec. 3.1, first the hybrid model for one investor introduced in Sec. 2.1 is extended to a market model, and the equilibrium prices are explicitly determined. Then information systems are considered, and information values corresponding to two alternative scenarios are defined and explicitly determined for them. In order to keep the representation clear, only the situations of theorem 3 and theorem 5 are more precisely dealt with, i.e. the basic hybrid model and unbiased, normally distributed estimators of the end-of-period prices[2] are presupposed.

3.1 Capital Market Equilibrium for Heterogeneous Expectations

This section covers a short presentation of Lintner's [1969] results. Starting-point is the hybrid model presented in Sec. 2.1 which is presupposed for each investor. As the individual data α, w, μ, Ω can be different from investor to investor, additional subcripts are necessary.

Altogether, m investors are considered $(m \in \mathbb{N})$. Each investor $k \in M = \{1, \ldots, m\}$ has an initial wealth $w_k \in \mathbb{R}$, an exponential utility function

---

[1] except in the two extreme cases that nobody or all investors are informed.

[2] or linear transformations of these prices, respectively.

$$u_k(g) = -e^{-\alpha_k g} \qquad \forall\, g \in \mathbb{R}$$

and prior starts from normally distributed end-of-period prices:[1]

(73) $\quad X \sim N(\mu_k, \Omega_k)$ for investor k .

The density corresponding to (73) is denoted by φ_k . If the investor chooses the portfolio vector:[2]

$$y_k = (y_{k1}, \ldots, y_{kn})^T \in \mathbb{R}^n$$

then analogously to (3)

(74) $$g_{k,v}(x, y_k) = w_k(1+r) + y_k^T(x - (1+r)v)$$

yields as end-of-period wealth dependent on x . The associated certainty equivalent yields analogously to (6):

(75) $$\upsilon_{\varphi_k}(g_{k,v}(X, y_k)) = w_k(1+r) + y_k^T(\mu_k - (1+r)v) - \frac{\alpha_k}{2} y_k^T \Omega_k y_k$$

The result function depends - via w_k - on k and, of course on the prices v at the beginning. The subscripts of g consider this. According to (10)

(76) $$y_k^* = \frac{1}{\alpha_k} \Omega_k^{-1}(\mu_k - (1+r)v)$$

results as optimal portfolio decision with the associated certainty equivalent:

(77) $$\upsilon_{\varphi_k}(g_{k,v}(X, y_k^*)) = w_k(1+r) + \frac{1}{2\alpha_k}(\mu_k - (1+r)v)^T \Omega_k^{-1}(\mu_k - (1+r)v)$$

In opposition to Sec. 2, now it is assumed that the prices v at the beginning are not exogeneously given, but represent equilibrium prices:

(78) $$\sum_{k=1}^{m} y_k^* = (1, \ldots, 1)^T =: \mathbb{1}$$

Hence, all investors together keep 100 % of each asset. (76) replaced in (78), yields

(79) $$\mathbb{1} = \sum_{k=1}^{m} \frac{1}{\alpha_k} \Omega_k^{-1}(\mu_k - (1+r)v)$$

Resolving v in (79), the well-known formula for the *equilibrium prices* is obtained:

(80) $$v = \frac{\mu_M - \alpha_M \Omega_M \mathbb{1}}{1 + r}$$

---

1) Ω_k is always assumed to be positive definite.

2) Again, y_{ki} is the fraction of asset i which the investor k keeps.

with the market quantities

(81) $\alpha_M := \left(\sum_{k=1}^{m} \alpha_k^{-1}\right)^{-1}$

(82) $\Omega_M := \left(\sum_{k=1}^{m} \frac{\alpha_M}{\alpha_k} \Omega_k^{-1}\right)^{-1}$

(83) $\mu_M := \Omega_M\left(\sum_{k=1}^{m} \frac{\alpha_M}{\alpha_k} \Omega_k^{-1} \mu_k\right)$

According to (76),(77), and (80)

(84) $y_k^* = \frac{1}{\alpha_k} \Omega_k^{-1} (\mu_k - \mu_M + \alpha_M \Omega_M \mathbb{1})$

(85) $v_{\varphi_k} (g_{k,v}(X,y_k^*)) = w_k (1+r) + \frac{1}{2\alpha_k}(\mu_k - \mu_M + \alpha_M\Omega_M \mathbb{1})^T\Omega_k^{-1}(\mu_k - \mu_M + \alpha_M\Omega_M \mathbb{1})$

are true. In order to determine his optimal portfolio, however, the investor does not need to know the market quantities α_M, Ω_M, and μ_M. As v can be observed, he can evaluate y_k^* according to (76) whereby he only needs to know his individual data α_k, Ω_k, and μ_k.

In special cases, the determination of the market quantities is simplified (see (81),(82),(83)):

- $\alpha_k = \alpha \quad \forall\, k \in M \Rightarrow \alpha_M = \frac{\alpha}{m}$
- $\mu_k = \mu \quad \forall\, k \in M \Rightarrow \mu_M = \mu$
- $\Omega_k = \Omega \quad \forall\, k \in M \Rightarrow \Omega_M = \Omega\, , \; \mu_M = \sum_{k=1}^{m} \frac{\alpha_M}{\alpha_k} \mu_k$

Especially, under the assumption of homogeneous expectations, hence, the market paramters μ_M and Ω_M are the same as the individual parameters. Then, according to (84),(85)

(86) $y_k^* = \frac{\alpha_M}{\alpha_k} \mathbb{1}$

(87) $v_{\varphi_k} (g_{k,v}(X,y_k^*)) = w_k (1+r) + \frac{\alpha_M^2}{2\alpha_k} \mathbb{1}^T \Omega\, \mathbb{1}$

The statement (86) corresponds to the *separation theorem:* The proportions of the optimal portfolio are independent of α_k and w_k, therefore the same for all investors. Each investor keeps a portion of the market portfolio determined by his risk aversion. In particular, for the case of homogeneous expectations, the following is true $(m > 1)$:

$$0 < y^*_{ki} = \frac{\alpha_M}{\alpha_k} < 1 \quad \forall\, i,k$$

i.e. the problematic special cases[1] are excluded.

The connection to the *Capital Asset Pricing Model* (CAPM) is given by (80) also in the general case of heterogeneous expectations which is here first of all interesting:

Let

$$R_i := \frac{X_i}{v_i} - 1 \qquad i = 1,\dots,n$$

$$R_M := \frac{\sum_j v_j R_j}{\sum_j v_j}$$

be the stochastic rates of return of the single assets or the market portfolio, respectively. According to (80), the following is true[2]

$$v_i = \frac{E_M X_i - \alpha_M \sum_j \mathrm{Cov}_M(X_i, X_j)}{1 + r} \qquad i = 1,\dots,n$$

$$r = E_M R_i - \alpha_M \sum_j v_j \ \mathrm{Cov}_M(R_i, R_j) = E_M R_i - \alpha_M \left[\sum_j v_j\right] \mathrm{Cov}_M(R_i, R_M)$$

or

(88) $$E_M R_i = r + \alpha_M \left[\sum_j v_j\right] \mathrm{Cov}_M(R_i, R_M) \Rightarrow$$

(89) $$E_M R_M = \frac{\sum_i v_i E_M R_i}{\sum_j v_j} = r + \alpha_M \sum_i v_i \ \mathrm{Cov}_M(R_i, R_M) = r + \alpha_M \left[\sum_i v_i\right] \mathrm{Var}_M(R_M)$$

Summarizing (88) and (89), then the basic equation of the CAPM results:

(90) $$E_M R_i = r + \beta_i (E_M R_M - r)$$

with

$$\beta_i := \frac{\mathrm{Cov}_M(R_i, R_M)}{\mathrm{Var}_M(R_M)}$$

---

1) short sales, 'corner'.

2) The subscript M indicates that the market expections (82),(83) are presupposed.

3.2 Information Systems

Let an information system Z be given which with prior normally distributed prices alway leads to posterior normally distributed prices (see Sec. 2.3). Let a group $N \subset M$ of investors be informed about the result z of Z, while the other investors $(M - N)$ remain uninformed.[1] The latter ones keep their prior expectations while the informed ones pass over to their corresponding posterior expectations. This leads to new equilibrium prices and to new optimal portfolio decisions of *all* investors.

Formally, this situation can best be described with the aid of a so-called *Null-information system* Z_o that always provides the message z_o.[2] The entire information activity then is a vector Z^N of random variables whose k-th component is the random variable Z_k^N the result of which investor k observes:

$$(91) \qquad Z^N := (Z_1^N, \ldots, Z_m^N)^T$$

with

$$(92) \qquad Z_k^N := \begin{cases} Z & \text{if} \quad k \in N \\ Z_o & \text{if} \quad k \notin N \end{cases} \qquad \forall\, k \in M$$

As usual, the results of random variables are denoted by lowercase letters:

$$(93) \qquad z^N := (z_1^N, \ldots, z_m^N)^T$$

$$(94) \qquad z_k^N := \begin{cases} z & \text{if} \quad k \in N \\ z_o & \text{if} \quad k \notin N \end{cases} \qquad \forall\, k \in M$$

Considerably more general information activities of the market participants can be described by (91) by allowing individually different information systems for each investor. However, it is renounced on this, because the resulting formula e.g. for the optimal portfolios are on the one hand rather complicated and hard to interpret, and on the other hand can numerically be evaluated only if one knows all individual data and the joint density of all random variables which can be excluded in practice.

---

1) The cases $N = \emptyset$ and $N = M$ are not excluded. In particular, the extreme cases insider information (N contains one element), and public information $(N = M)$ are interesting.

2) Z_o is a constant random variable; z_o can have any value where z_o := 'no information' is obvious.

As in Sec. 2.3, the distribution of Z may be described by a likelihood density $f_x(z)$. Let this one be known to, and accepted by each investor.[1] As well the marginal densities

$$(95) \qquad f_k(z) := \int f_x(z)\varphi_k(x)\,dx$$

as the posterior densities

$$(96) \qquad \varphi_{k,z_k^N}(x) = \begin{cases} \dfrac{f_x(z)\varphi_k(x)}{f_k(z)} & \text{if} \quad k\in N \\ \varphi_k(x) & \text{if} \quad k\notin N \end{cases}$$

however, are generally different from investor to investor.

The posterior distributions are assumed as normal distributions

$$(97) \qquad X\Big|_{Z_k^N=z_k^N} \sim N(\mu_k(z_k^N),\Omega_k(z_k^N)) \quad \text{for investor} \quad k$$

where

$$(98) \qquad \mu_k(z_k^N) = \begin{cases} \mu_k(z) & \text{if} \quad k\in N \\ \mu_k & \text{if} \quad k\notin N \end{cases}$$

$$(99) \qquad \Omega_k(z_k^N) = \begin{cases} \Omega_k(z) & \text{if} \quad k\in N \\ \Omega_k & \text{if} \quad k\notin N \end{cases}$$

The posterior formulas[2] corresponding to (76),(80) to (85) are (the risk aversion of the market remains unchanged):

$$(100) \qquad \Omega_M(z^N) = \left(\sum_{k=1}^{m} \frac{\alpha_M}{\alpha_k}(\Omega_k(z_k^N))^{-1}\right)^{-1} = \left(\sum_{k\in N} \frac{\alpha_M}{\alpha_k}(\Omega_k(z))^{-1} + \sum_{k\notin N}\frac{\alpha_M}{\alpha_k}\Omega_k^{-1}\right)^{-1}$$

$$(101) \qquad \mu_M(z^N) = \Omega_M(z^N)\left(\sum_{k=1}^{m} \frac{\alpha_M}{\alpha_k}(\Omega_k(z_k^N))^{-1}\mu_k(z_k^N)\right)$$

$$= \Omega_M(z^N)\left(\sum_{k\in N} \frac{\alpha_M}{\alpha_k}(\Omega_k(z))^{-1}\mu_k(z) + \sum_{k\notin N}\frac{\alpha_M}{\alpha_k}\Omega_k^{-1}\mu_k\right)$$

---

1) For some of the following statements it would be sufficient to make this assumption only for the informed investors. If one and the same information system is evaluated differently by different informed investors, then this is equivalent to the presupposition of different information systems and leads to the above addressed difficulties.

2) For $N=\emptyset$ the prior expressions result.

(102) $$v(z^N) = \frac{\mu_M(z^N) - \alpha_M \, \Omega_M(z^N)\, 1\!\!1}{1+r}$$

(103) $$y_k^*(z_k^N, v(z^N)) = \frac{1}{\alpha_k} \, (\Omega_k(z_k^N))^{-1} (\mu_k(z_k^N) - (1+r)v(z^N))$$

$$= \frac{1}{\alpha_k} \, (\Omega_k(z_k^N))^{-1} (\mu_k(z_k^N) - \mu_M(z^N) + \alpha_M \Omega_M(z^N)\, 1\!\!1)$$

(104) $$\upsilon_{\varphi_{k,z_k^N}}(g_{k,v(z^N)}(X, y_k^*(z_k^N, v(z^N)))) =$$

$$w_k(1+r) + \frac{1}{2\alpha_k}(\mu_k(z_k^N) - \mu_M(z^N) + \alpha_M \Omega_M(z^N)\, 1\!\!1)^T \, (\Omega_k(z_k^N))^{-1}$$

$$(\mu_k(z_k^N) - \mu_M(z^N) + \alpha_M \Omega_M(z^N)\, 1\!\!1)$$

In order to determine his posterior optimal portfolio (103), the investor k needs to know besides his individual data only the (observable) equilibrium prices $v(z^N)$. Although it is assumed that the expectations of the uninformed investors do not change, also their portfolio decisions change because of the changed prices (see (103)).

Especially handy results yield for the information system introduced in theorem 3:

Theorem 9:

Let the information system Z about whose result z the group N of investors is informed fulfill the presuppositions of theorem 3. Let

(105) $$\alpha_N := \left(\sum_{k \in N} \alpha_k^{-1}\right)^{-1}$$

(106) $$d_N := \frac{\alpha_M}{\alpha_N}$$

then the following statements are true:

(107) $$\Omega_k(z) = (T^T \Sigma^{-1} T + \Omega_k^{-1})^{-1}$$

(108) $$\mu_k(z) = \Omega_k(z)(T^T \Sigma^{-1} z + \Omega_k^{-1} \mu_k)$$

(109) $$\Omega_M(z^N) = (d_N T^T \Sigma^{-1} T + \Omega_M^{-1})^{-1}$$

(110) $$\mu_M(z^N) = \Omega_M(z^N)(d_N T^T \Sigma^{-1} z + \Omega_M^{-1} \mu_M) \; .$$

(107),(108) immediately follow from (42), and (109),(110) then follow from (82),(83),(100),(101).

According to (43), then it is easy to determine the marginal distribution

(111) $\quad z \sim N(T\mu_k, T\Omega_k T^T + \Sigma)$ for investor k .

It is remarkable that the covariances (107),(109) are independent of z , and that the expectations (108),(110) are linear functions of z .

(105) specifies the risk aversion of the group N of informed investors, and d_N denotes the part of informed investors - measured by the risk aversion.[1]

For published information $d_N = 1$ is true, while $d_N \approx 0$ corresponds to insider information by which the market quantities are not considerably influenced: $\Omega_M(z^N) \approx \Omega_M$, $\mu_M(z^N) \approx \mu_M$, $v(z^N) \approx v$ according to (80),(102),(110).

The vector of the price changes $v(z^N)-v$ is in a first approximation proportional to d_N , for according to (80),(102),(109),(110), it holds

$$(112) \qquad v(z^N) = \frac{1}{1+r} (d_N T^T\Sigma^{-1}T+\Omega^{-1})^{-1}(d_N T^T\Sigma^{-1}z+\Omega_M^{-1}\mu_M-\alpha_M 1\!\!1)$$

$$= v + \frac{d_N}{1+r} (d_N T^T\Sigma^{-1}T+\Omega_M^{-1})^{-1}T^T\Sigma^{-1}(z-(1+r)Tv) \;.$$

According to (112) also the (observable) equlibrium prices are a linear function of z . Determining z with the aid of the prices $v(z^N)$, however, is possible for an uninformed investor only if he knows d_N and Ω_M . According to (82), the individual risk aversion and covariance matrices are required for this which are hardly known in practice.[2] Therefore, generally the uninformed investors cannot

---

[1] If α_k^{-1} and w_k are proportional (see example 3 in Sec. 2.4.2), then $d_N = (\sum_{k\in N} w_k)/(\sum_{k\in M} w_k)$.

[2] However, under the assumption of homogeneous expectations, such a determination is possible, and the presumption of uninformed investors is correspondingly problematic, see Grossmann [1976,1978].

subsequently deduce the information z. Correspondingly, the assumption that the uninformed investors do not change their expectations can in a first approximation be confirmed especially when - as here - the equilibrium prices were considered as results of the expectations and not as information influencing the expectations, see the literature cited in Sec. 1.4 regarding the information efficiency and, in particular, Hellwig [1980].

3.3 Information Evaluation

The market model introduced in Sec. 3.1 is assumed. Further, let an information system Z as considered in Sec. 3.2 be given which always leads to posterior normally distributed end-of-period prices.[1] The expected value of information for investor k is defined analogously to (47).[2] Now it depends on the extent of the price changes, i.e. on the group of investors to be informed, and on whether investor k has already realized his prior optimal portfolio before information access or not:

Let $k \in M$, $N \subset M$ and Z be an information system as considered in Sec. 3.2:

The *expected value of information* (EVI(k,N)) for investor k, if N is informed, is defined as the solution of the equation

(113) $$\max_{y_k} E_{\varphi_k} u_k(g_{k,v}(X,y_k))$$
$$= E_{f_k}\left(\max_{y_k} E_{\varphi_{k,z_k^N}} u_k(g_{k,v(z^N)}(X,y_k) - \mathrm{EVI}(k,N))\right)$$

The *expected total value of information* (ETVI(k,N)) for investor k, if N is informed, is defined as the solution of the equation

(114) $$\max_{y_k} E_{\varphi_k} u_k(g_{k,v}(X,y_k))$$
$$= E_{f_k}\left(\max_{y_k} E_{\varphi_{k,z_k^N}} u_k(g_{k,v(z^N)}(X,y_k)+(1+r)y_k^{*T}(v(z^N)-v) - \mathrm{ETVI}(k,N))\right)$$

The EVI does not consider any profits (or losses) because of the equilibrium price changes caused by the information activity. This

1) This presumption is not necessary for defining the information values, but for proving the following results.

2) A definition as selling value again leads to the same result, see (48).

corresponds to the situation that the investor k did not riskily invest any amounts before information access. He compares the two situations 'realization of the prior optimal portfolio before information access' and 'realization of the optimal[1] portfolio after information access'. Conversely, (114) corresponds to a portfolio revision model. The investor already keeps the prior optimal portfolio y_k^* and will revise it after information access, correspondingly. Then this leads to the profit (or loss) $y_k^{*T}(v(z^N)-v)$. As this already becomes available at the beginning of the period, and as all other payments are referred to the end of the period, this profit is multiplied by $1+r$.

One might object to the use of the prior optimal portfolio on the righthand side of (114) that the investor should take advantage of the information 'an information influencing the equilibrium prices will arrive'. The in this sence optimal portfolio does not have to be the same as y_k^* . Correspondingly, it should additionally be optimized on the righthand side of (114) with respect to this decision variable whereby also the equilibrium prices v would change. By this, a third definition for the information value would result. For two reasons, this without any doubt interesting way is in the following not taken. On the one hand the already now quite complicated results - as it will show - will become still harder to follow up. On the other hand, the information value defined here can anyway only be interpreted in a limited way pragmatically in the sense of an information decision to be made by the investor. For the two situations 'nobody obtains any information' and 'a defined group N obtains information' are compared from the viewpoint of the considered investor. Of course, in reality the investor cannot choose between these two situations. At best, he can decide about his own information activity which corresponds to the situation in Sec. 2. If, however, no decision has to be made, but only the advantage of the one situation against the other shall be quantified, then improving the investment result by anticipating the information influenced price changes is not possible.

---

1) if $k \in N$, it concerns the posterior optimal portfolio, otherwise $(k \notin N)$ the portfolio optimal with respect to the prior data and the new equilibrium prices.

In both cases (113),(114), the expressions on the lefthand side are maximized by y_k^* (see (84)) and on the righthand side by $y_k^*(z_k^N, v(z^N))$ (see (103)). Analogously to (48) it immediately follows:

(115) $$EVI(k,N) = A(k,N) - A(k,\emptyset)$$

(116) $$ETVI(k,N) = B(k,N) - B(k,\emptyset)$$

where (see (84),(102),(104))

(117) $$A(k,N) := u_k^{-1}\left(E_{f_k} u_k\left(\upsilon_{\varphi_{k,z_k^N}}[g_{k,v(z^N)}(X, y_k^*(z_k^N, v(z^N)))] - w_k(1+r)\right)\right)$$

$$= \frac{-1}{\alpha_k} \ln E_{f_k} \exp\left[-\frac{1}{2}(\mu_k(z_k^N) - \mu_M(z^N) + \alpha_M\Omega_M(z^N)1|)^T\right.$$

$$\left.(\Omega_k(z_k^N))^{-1}(\mu_k(z_k^N) - \mu_M(z^N) + \alpha_M\Omega_M(z^N)1|)\right]$$

(118) $$B(k,N) := u_k^{-1}\left(E_{f_k} u_k\left(\upsilon_{\varphi_{k,z_k^N}}[g_{k,v(z^N)}(X, y_k^*(z_k^N, v(z^N)))]\right.\right.$$

$$\left.\left.- w_k(1+r) + (1+r)y_k^{*T} v(z^N)\right)\right)$$

$$= \frac{-1}{\alpha_k} \ln E_{f_k} \exp\left[-\frac{1}{2}(\mu_k(z_k^N) - \mu_M(z^N) + \alpha_M\Omega_M(z^N)1|)^T\right.$$

$$(\Omega_k(z_k^N))^{-1}(\mu_k(z_k^N) - \mu_M(z^N) + \alpha_M\Omega_M(z^N)1|)$$

$$\left.- (\mu_k - \mu_M + \alpha_M\Omega_M 1|)^T \Omega_k^{-1}(\mu_M(z^N) - \alpha_M\Omega_M(z^N)1|)\right]$$

By (113) and (114), the transition from the situation 'nobody is informed' to the situation 'the group N is informed' is evaluated - from the viewpoint of investor k. It might be interesting to perform also other comparisons, e.g. to confront under pragmatic viewpoints 'N is informed' and 'N ∪ {k} is informed' ($k \notin N$). Defining generally as EVI (k,N_1,N_2) or ETVI (k,N_1,N_2) the value which the transition from the situation 'N_1 is informed' to the situation 'N_2 is informed' has for investor k, in analogy to (113) or (114), then (see (115), (116))

(119) $$EVI(K,N_1,N_2) = A(k,N_2) - A(k,N_1) = EVI(k,N_2) - EVI(k,N_1)$$

(120) $$ETVI(k,N_1,N_2) = B(k,N_2) - B(k,N_1) = ETVI(k,N_2) - ETVI(k,N_1)$$

result.

Knowing the functions A,B or the information values (115),(116) these general information values, therefore, can immediately be determined. Hence, in the following, only the values (115),(116) are analyzed.

(115),(116) can also be determined for $k \notin N$, but in this case cannot at all be interpreted as pragmatic information values - from the viewpoint of investor k - because there does not exist an information problem for k. The EVI or ETVI then only specifies the advantage (or disadvantage) which results for investor k from the changed prices from the viewpoint of his unchanged expectations.[1] If the investor already keeps his prior optimal portfolio, then its certainty equivalent is for $k \notin N$ not changed by price changes, i.e. by the information activity, the decision situation can at most improve for him.[2] This is also true for $k \in N$:

Theorem 10:

Let $k \in M$, $N \subset M$, and Z be an information system. Under the presumptions made in Sec. 3.1, 3.2

(121) $\quad ETVI(k,N) \geq 0$

Proof:

The following is true (see (74)):

$$g_{k,v(z^N)}(x,y_k^*) + (1+r)y_k^{*T} v(z^N) = w_k(1+r) + y_k^{*T} x$$

$$= w_k(1+r) + y_k^{*T}(x - (1+r)v) + (1+r)y_k^{*T} v = g_{k,v}(X,y_k^*) + (1+r)y_k^{*T} v$$

This expression is independent of z, and (118) gives because of

$$\upsilon_{\varphi_{k,z_k^N}}\left[g_{k,v(z^N)}(X,y_k^*)\right] \leq \upsilon_{\varphi_{k,z_k^N}}\left[g_{k,v(z^N)}(X,y_k^*(z_k^N,v(z^N)))\right]$$

the result

$$B(k,N) \geq B(k,\emptyset) \quad . \qquad \square$$

---

1) The distribution of the information effected changed prices at the beginning of the period is described for investor k by f_k. Also the uninformed investor knows the information system, but not the realized message.

2) However, this improvement is first of all founded on his unchanged information level which is obsolete against one part of the market (N).

A corresponding result is not to be expected for the EVI as the following, however unrealistic example shows:

Example 5:

Let Z be a perfect information system, i.e. Z supplies as message the true end-of-period prices. Then the posterior distributions are in fact not normal, but degenerate; however, all quoted statements remain analogously valid. If the result of Z is published $(N = M)$, then as new equilibrium prices obviously such values result which give for any - now safe - asset the same rate of return r. But this rate of return can also be reached at once without information, i.e. one obtains

$$EVI(k,M) < 0 \quad ^{1)}$$

for this example. It will show (see (159)) that this result can also occur for imperfect information systems as described in theorem 3. Decreasing risk decreases the risk premium attainable by the investor.

It immediately follows from (117),(118) for $N = \emptyset$:

$$(122) \qquad A(k,\emptyset) = \frac{1}{2\alpha_k}(\mu_k - \mu_M + \alpha_M \Omega_M 1\!\!1)^T \Omega_k^{-1} (\mu_k - \mu_M + \alpha_M \Omega_M 1\!\!1)$$

$$(123) \qquad B(k,\emptyset) = \frac{1}{2\alpha_k}(\mu_k - \mu_M + \alpha_M \Omega_M 1\!\!1)^T \Omega_k^{-1} (\mu_k + \mu_M - \alpha_M \Omega_M 1\!\!1)$$

For the information system introduced in theorem 3, the functions A,B can also be determined for $N \neq \emptyset$.

Theorem 11:

Let $k \in M$, $N \subset M$, $N \neq \emptyset$,

$$a := \mu_k - \mu_M + \alpha_M \Omega_M 1\!\!1$$

and Z be an information system according to theorem 3, then

a) if $k \in N$:

$$(124) \qquad A(k,N) = \frac{1}{2\alpha_k} \ln \frac{|T\Omega_k T^T + \Sigma|\,|d_N^2 T\Omega_M \Omega_k^{-1} \Omega_M T^T + \Sigma|}{|d_N T\Omega_M T^T + \Sigma|^2}$$

$$+ \frac{1}{2\alpha_k} a^T (\Omega_k + d_N^2 \Omega_M T^T \Sigma^{-1} T \Omega_M)^{-1} a$$

1) The equality is excluded if prior a real portfolio is optimal $(\mu_k \neq (1+r)v)$.

(125) $$B(k,N) = \frac{1}{2\alpha_k} \ln \frac{|T\Omega_k T^T + \Sigma| \, |d_N^2 T\Omega_M \Omega_k^{-1}\Omega_M T^T + \Sigma|}{|d_N T\Omega_M T^T + \Sigma|^2} + B(k,\emptyset)$$

b) if $k \notin N$:

(126) $$A(k,N) = \frac{1}{2\alpha_k} \ln| (T\Omega_k T^T+\Sigma)(d_N T\Omega_M T^T+\Sigma)^{-1}(Td_N^2\Omega_M\Omega_k^{-1}\Omega_M T^T)(d_N T\Omega_M T^T+\Sigma)^{-1}+Id_t| +$$

$$+ \frac{1}{2\alpha_k} a^T \Omega_M^{-1}[\Omega_M^{-1}+d_N T^T\Sigma^{-1}T)\Omega_k(\Omega_M^{-1}+d_N T^T\Sigma^{-1}T) +$$

$$+ d_N^2(T^T\Sigma^{-1}T\Omega_k T^T\Sigma^{-1}T+T^T\Sigma^{-1}T)]^{-1}\Omega_M^{-1}a$$

(127) $$B(k,N) = \frac{1}{2\alpha_k} \ln| (T\Omega_k T^T+\Sigma)(d_N T\Omega_M T^T+\Sigma)^{-1}(Td_N^2\Omega_M\Omega_k^{-1}\Omega_M T^T)(d_N T\Omega_M T^T+\Sigma)^{-1}+Id_t| +$$

$$+ \frac{1}{2\alpha_k} a^T T^T[T\Omega_k T^T+\Sigma+(d_N T\Omega_M T^T+\Sigma)(Td_N^2\Omega_M\Omega_k^{-1}\Omega_M T^T)^{-1}(d_N T\Omega_M T^T+\Sigma)]^{-1}Ta+B(k,\emptyset)$$

Proof:

According to (107),(109), the posterior covariance matrices are independent of z. To make this clear $\Omega_k(z)$ is denoted by $\bar{\Omega}_k$ and $\Omega_M(z^N)$ by $\bar{\Omega}_M$:

$$\bar{\Omega}_k := \Omega_k(z) \qquad \bar{\Omega}_M := \Omega_M(z^N)$$

From (111),(117),(118) it follows:

(128) $$A(k,N) = \frac{-1}{\alpha_k} \ln\left[(2\pi)^{-t/2}|T\Omega_k T^T+\Sigma|^{-1/2} \int e^{-a_{k,N}(z)} dz\right]$$

(129) $$B(k,N) = \frac{-1}{\alpha_k} \ln\left[(2\pi)^{-t/2}|T\Omega_k T^T+\Sigma|^{-1/2} \int e^{-b_{k,N}(z)} dz\right]$$

with

$$a_{k,N}(z) = \frac{1}{2}(z-T\mu_k)^T(T\Omega_k T^T+\Sigma)^{-1}(z-T\mu_k)$$

$$+ \begin{cases} \frac{1}{2}(\mu_k(z)-\mu_M(z^N)+\alpha_M\bar{\Omega}_M 1|)^T\bar{\Omega}_k^{-1}(\mu_k(z)-\mu_M(z^N)+\alpha_M\bar{\Omega}_M 1|) & \text{if } k \in N \\ \frac{1}{2}(\mu_k-\mu_M(z^N)+\alpha_M\bar{\Omega}_M 1|)^T\Omega_k^{-1}(\mu_k-\mu_M(z^N)+\alpha_M\bar{\Omega}_M 1|) & \text{if } k \notin N \end{cases}$$

$$b_{k,N}(z) = a_{k,N}(z) + (\mu_k-\mu_M+\alpha_M\Omega_M 1|)^T\Omega_k^{-1}(\mu_M(z^N)-\alpha_M\bar{\Omega}_M 1|)$$

At first a) is proven:

Let $k \in N$, according to (107),(108) (see (162)) the following is true ($TT^T \in \mathbb{R}^{(t,t)}$ is invertible because of $\operatorname{rank}(T) = t$):

(130) $$(\mu_k(z)-\mu_M(z^N)+\alpha_M\bar{\Omega}_M 1\!\!1)^T \bar{\Omega}_k^{-1}(\mu_k(z)-\mu_M(z^N)+\alpha_M\bar{\Omega}_M 1\!\!1)$$

$$= (\bar{\Omega}_k(T^T\Sigma^{-1}T(T^T(TT^T)^{-1}z)+\Omega_k^{-1}\mu_k)-(\mu_M(z^N)-\alpha_M\bar{\Omega}_M 1\!\!1))^T \bar{\Omega}_k^{-1}$$

$$(\bar{\Omega}_k(T^T\Sigma^{-1}T(T^T(TT^T)^{-1}z)+\Omega_k^{-1}\mu_k)-(\mu_M(z^N)-\alpha_M\bar{\Omega}_M 1\!\!1))$$

$$= (T^T(TT^T)^{-1}z-\mu_M(z^N)+\alpha_M\bar{\Omega}_M 1\!\!1)^T T^T\Sigma^{-1}T(T^T(TT^T)^{-1}z-\mu_M(z^N)+\alpha_M\bar{\Omega}_M 1\!\!1)$$

$$+ (\mu_k-\mu_M(z^N)+\alpha_M\bar{\Omega}_M 1\!\!1)^T \Omega_k^{-1}(\mu_k-\mu_M(z^N)+\alpha_M\bar{\Omega}_M 1\!\!1)$$

$$- (T^T(TT^T)^{-1}z-\mu_k)^T \Omega_k^{-1}\bar{\Omega}_k T^T\Sigma^{-1}T(T^T(TT^T)^{-1}z-\mu_k)$$

Because of (see (109),(110)):

(131) $$\mu_M(z^N) = \bar{\Omega}_M\Omega_M^{-1}\mu_M + \bar{\Omega}_M d_N T^T\Sigma^{-1}T(T^T(TT^T)^{-1}z)$$

$$= \bar{\Omega}_M\Omega_M^{-1}\mu_M + T^T(TT^T)^{-1}z-\bar{\Omega}_M\Omega_M^{-1}T^T(TT^T)^{-1}z$$

and (see (167)):

(132) $$\Omega_k^{-1}\bar{\Omega}_k T^T\Sigma^{-1}T = T^T(T\Omega_k T^T+\Sigma)^{-1}T$$

it follows from (130):

(133) $$2a_{k,N}(z) = (T^T(TT^T)^{-1}z-\mu_M+\alpha_M\Omega_M 1\!\!1)^T \Omega_M^{-1}\bar{\Omega}_M T^T\Sigma^{-1}T\bar{\Omega}_M\Omega_M^{-1}$$

$$(T^T(TT^T)^{-1}z-\mu_M+\alpha_M\Omega_M 1\!\!1) + (\mu_k-\mu_M(z^N)+\alpha_M\bar{\Omega}_M 1\!\!1)^T \Omega_k^{-1}(\mu_k-\mu_M(z^N)+\alpha_M\bar{\Omega}_M 1\!\!1)$$

The following equations are immediately understandable:

(134) $$\mu_k-\mu_M(z^N)+\alpha_M\bar{\Omega}_M 1\!\!1 = (\mu_k-\mu_M+\alpha_M\Omega_M 1\!\!1) + (\mu_M-\mu_M(z^N)-\alpha_M(\Omega_M-\bar{\Omega}_M)1\!\!1)$$

(135) $$\mu_M-\mu_M(z^N) = -d_N\bar{\Omega}_M T^T\Sigma^{-1}(z-T\mu_M) \qquad \text{(see (110))}$$

(136) $$\Omega_M-\bar{\Omega}_M = d_N\bar{\Omega}_M T^T\Sigma^{-1}T\Omega_M \qquad \text{(see (109))}$$

(137) $$\Omega_M^{-1}\bar{\Omega}_M T^T\Sigma^{-1}T = T^T\Sigma^{-1}T - d_N T^T\Sigma^{-1}T\bar{\Omega}_M T^T\Sigma^{-1}T = T^T\Sigma^{-1}T\bar{\Omega}_M\Omega_M^{-1},$$

which yields

(138) $$\Omega_M^{-1}\bar{\Omega}_M T^T\Sigma^{-1}T\bar{\Omega}_M\Omega_M^{-1} = T^T\Sigma^{-1}T\bar{\Omega}_M\Omega_M^{-1}[T^T(TT^T)^{-1}\Sigma(TT^T)^{-1}T]\Omega_M^{-1}\bar{\Omega}_M T^T\Sigma^{-1}T$$

This yields for (133):

(139) $$2a_{k,N}(z) = (z-T(\mu_M-\alpha_M\Omega_M 1\!|))^T$$

$$\Sigma^{-1}T\bar{\Omega}_M\Omega_M^{-1}[T^T(TT^T)^{-1}\Sigma(TT^T)^{-1}T]\Omega_M^{-1}\bar{\Omega}_M T^T\Sigma^{-1}(z-T(\mu_M-\alpha_M\Omega_M 1\!|))$$

$$+ (\mu_k-\mu_M+\alpha_M\Omega_M 1\!|)^T\Omega_k^{-1}(\mu_k-\mu_M+\alpha_M\Omega_M 1\!|)$$

$$+ (\mu_M-\mu_M(z^N)-\alpha_M(\Omega_M-\bar{\Omega}_M)1\!|)^T\Omega_k^{-1}(\mu_M-\mu_M(z^N)-\alpha_M(\Omega_M-\bar{\Omega}_M)1\!|)$$

$$+ 2(\mu_k-\mu_M+\alpha_M\Omega_M 1\!|)^T\Omega_k^{-1}(\mu_M-\mu_M(z^N)-\alpha_M(\Omega_M-\bar{\Omega}_M)1\!|)$$

$$= (z-T(\mu_M-\alpha_M\Omega_M 1\!|))^T C(z-T(\mu_M-\alpha_M\Omega_M 1\!|))$$

$$+ (\mu_k-\mu_M+\alpha_M\Omega_M 1\!|)^T\Omega_k^{-1}(\mu_k-\mu_M-\alpha_M\Omega_M 1\!|)$$

$$+ 2(\mu_k-\mu_M+\alpha_M\Omega_M 1\!|)^T\Omega_k^{-1}(\mu_M-\mu_M(z^N)-\alpha_M(\Omega_M-\bar{\Omega}_M)1\!|)$$

with

(140) $$C := \Sigma^{-1}T\bar{\Omega}_M\Omega_M^{-1}[T^T(TT^T)^{-1}\Sigma(TT^T)^{-1}T]\Omega_M^{-1}\bar{\Omega}_M T^T\Sigma^{-1} + d_N^2\Sigma^{-1}T\bar{\Omega}_M\Omega_k^{-1}\bar{\Omega}_M T^T\Sigma^{-1}$$

C is positive definite, as the first term is positive semidefinite and the second one positive definite (see (163)). Because of (see (167))

(141) $$\Sigma^{-1}T\bar{\Omega}_M\Omega_M^{-1} = \Sigma^{-1}T - d_N\Sigma^{-1}T\bar{\Omega}_M T^T\Sigma^{-1}T = \Sigma^{-1}(\Sigma-d_N T\bar{\Omega}_M T^T)\Sigma^{-1}T$$

$$= \Sigma^{-1}(\Sigma-T(d_N^{-1}\Omega_M^{-1}+T^T\Sigma^{-1}T)^{-1}T^T)\Sigma^{-1}T = (d_N T\Omega_M T^T+\Sigma)^{-1}T$$

it yields in (140):

(142) $$C = (d_N T\Omega_M T^T+\Sigma)^{-1}(d_N^2 T\Omega_M\Omega_k^{-1}\Omega_M T^T+\Sigma)(d_N T\Omega_M T^T+\Sigma)^{-1}$$

According to (139)

$$2b_{k,N}(z) = (z-T(\mu_M-\alpha_M\Omega_M 1\!|))^T C(z-T(\mu_M-\alpha_M\Omega_M 1\!|))$$

$$+ (\mu_k-\mu_M+\alpha_M\Omega_M 1\!|)^T\Omega_k^{-1}(\mu_k-\mu_M+\alpha_M\Omega_M 1\!|) + 2(\mu_k-\mu_M+\alpha_M\Omega_M 1\!|)^T\Omega_k^{-1}(\mu_M-\alpha_M\Omega_M 1\!|)$$

$$= (z-T(\mu_M-\alpha_M\Omega_M 1\!|))^T C(z-T(\mu_M-\alpha_M\Omega_M 1\!|)) + (\mu_k-\mu_M+\alpha_M\Omega_M 1\!|)^T\Omega_k^{-1}(\mu_k+\mu_M-\alpha_M\Omega_M 1\!|)$$

and (125) immediately follows from (123),(129),(142):

$$B(k,N) = \frac{-1}{\alpha_k} \ell n \left[|T\Omega_k T^T + \Sigma|^{-1/2} |C|^{-1/2} \right] + B(k,\emptyset)$$

According to (135),(136),(139)

(143) $$a_{k,N}(z) = \frac{1}{2}(t - T(\mu_M - \alpha_M \Omega_M \mathbb{1}))^T C (t - T(\mu_M - \alpha_M \Omega_M \mathbb{1}))$$

$$+ \frac{1}{2}(\mu_k - \mu_M + \alpha_M \Omega_M \mathbb{1})^T \Omega_k^{-1} (\mu_k - \mu_M + \alpha_M \Omega_M \mathbb{1})$$

$$- d_N (\mu_k - \mu_M + \alpha_M \Omega_M \mathbb{1})^T \Omega_k^{-1} \bar{\Omega}_M T^T \Sigma^{-1} (z - T(\mu_M - \alpha_M \Omega_M \mathbb{1}))$$

$$= z^T \frac{C}{2} z - z^T \dot{c}_1 + \frac{c_0}{2}$$

with

(144) $$c_1 = d_N \Sigma^{-1} T \bar{\Omega}_M \Omega_k^{-1} (\mu_k - \mu_m + \alpha_M \Omega_M \mathbb{1}) + CT(\mu_M - \alpha_M \Omega_M \mathbb{1})$$

(145) $$c_0 = (\mu_M - \alpha_M \Omega_M \mathbb{1})^T T^T C T (\mu_M - \alpha_M \Omega_M \mathbb{1})$$

$$+ 2 d_N (\mu_k - \mu_M + \alpha_M \Omega_M \mathbb{1})^T \Omega_k^{-1} \bar{\Omega}_M T^T \Sigma^{-1} T (\mu_M - \alpha_M \Omega_M \mathbb{1})$$

$$+ (\mu_k - \mu_M + \alpha_M \Omega_M \mathbb{1})^T \Omega_k^{-1} (\mu_k - \mu_M + \alpha_M \Omega_M \mathbb{1})$$

According to (128) (see (172)):

(146) $$A(k,N) = \frac{1}{2\alpha_k} \ell n \left[|T\Omega_k T^T + \Sigma| |C| \right] + \frac{1}{2\alpha_k} (c_0 - c_1^T C^{-1} c_1)$$

where according to (144),(145):

(147) $$c_0 - c_1 C^{-1} c_1 = 2 d_N (\mu_k - \mu_M + \alpha_M \Omega_M \mathbb{1})^T \Omega_k^{-1} \bar{\Omega}_M T^T \Sigma^{-1} T (\mu_M - \alpha_M \Omega_M \mathbb{1})$$

$$+ (\mu_k - \mu_M + \alpha_M \Omega_M \mathbb{1})^T \Omega_k^{-1} (\mu_k - \mu_M + \alpha_M \Omega_M \mathbb{1})$$

$$- 2 d_N (\mu_k - \mu_M + \alpha_M \Omega_M \mathbb{1})^T \Omega_k^{-1} \bar{\Omega}_M T^T \Sigma^{-1} T (\mu_M - \alpha_M \Omega_M \mathbb{1})$$

$$- d_N^2 (\mu_k - \mu_M + \alpha_M \Omega_M \mathbb{1})^T \Omega_k^{-1} \bar{\Omega}_M T^T \Sigma^{-1} C^{-1} \Sigma^{-1} T \bar{\Omega}_M \Omega_k^{-1} (\mu_k - \mu_M + \alpha_M \Omega_M \mathbb{1})$$

$$= (\mu_k - \mu_M + \alpha_M \Omega_M \mathbb{1})^T D (\mu_k - \mu_M + \alpha_M \Omega_M \mathbb{1})$$

with

$$D := \Omega_k^{-1} - d_N^2\Omega_k^{-1}\bar{\Omega}_M T^T\Sigma^{-1}C^{-1}\Sigma^{-1}T\bar{\Omega}_M\Omega_k^{-1}$$

$$= \Omega_k^{-1}\Omega_M[\Omega_M^{-1}\Omega_k\Omega_M^{-1} - d_N^2(\Omega_M^{-1}\bar{\Omega}_M T^T\Sigma^{-1})C^{-1}(\Sigma^{-1}T\bar{\Omega}_M\Omega_M^{-1})]\Omega_M\Omega_k^{-1}$$

$$= \Omega_k^{-1}\Omega_M[\Omega_M^{-1}\Omega_k\Omega_M^{-1} - d_N^2 T^T(d_N^2 T\Omega_M\Omega_k^{-1}\Omega_M T^T + \Sigma)^{-1}T]\Omega_M\Omega_k^{-1} \qquad \text{(see (141),(142))}$$

$$= \Omega_k^{-1}\Omega_M[\Omega_M^{-1}\Omega_k\Omega_M^{-1} - T^T(T\Omega_M\Omega_k^{-1}\Omega_M T^T + d_N^{-2}\Sigma)^{-1}T]\Omega_M\Omega_k^{-1}$$

$$= \Omega_k^{-1}\Omega_M[\Omega_M^{-1}\Omega_k\Omega_M^{-1} - \Omega_M^{-1}\Omega_k\Omega_M^{-1}(\Omega_M^{-1}\Omega_k\Omega_M^{-1} + d_N^2 T^T\Sigma^{-1}T)^{-1}d_N^2 T^T\Sigma^{-1}T]\Omega_M\Omega_k^{-1}$$

(see (167))

$$= \Omega_k^{-1}\Omega_M[\Omega_M^{-1}\Omega_k\Omega_M^{-1}(\Omega_M^{-1}\Omega_k\Omega_M^{-1} + d_N^2 T^T\Sigma^{-1}T)^{-1}\Omega_M^{-1}\Omega_k\Omega_M^{-1}]\Omega_M\Omega_k^{-1}$$

$$= \Omega_M^{-1}(\Omega_M^{-1}\Omega_k\Omega_M^{-1} + d_N^2 T^T\Sigma^{-1}T)^{-1}\Omega_M^{-1}$$

and (142) follows from (146),(147). With that, part a) of theorem 11 is proven.

Let now $k \notin N$. First, (126) is shown. Because of (135),(136) with the abbreviation

$$b := T^T(TT^T)^{-1}z - \mu_M + \alpha_M\Omega_M 1\!\!1$$

for $a_{k,N}(z)$:

(148) $$2a_{k,N}(z) = (a - d_N\bar{\Omega}_M T^T\Sigma^{-1}Tb)^T\Omega_k^{-1}(a - d_N\bar{\Omega}_M T^T\Sigma^{-1}Tb)$$

$$+ (a-b)^T T^T(T\Omega_k T^T + \Sigma)^{-1}T(a-b)$$

$$= a^T[\Omega_k^{-1} + T^T(T\Omega_k T^T + \Sigma)^{-1}T]a + (Tb)^T[d_N^2\Sigma^{-1}T\bar{\Omega}_M\Omega_k^{-1}\bar{\Omega}_M T^T\Sigma^{-1} + (T\Omega_k T^T + \Sigma)^{-1}](Tb)$$

$$- 2a^T[d_N\Omega_k^{-1}\bar{\Omega}_M T^T\Sigma^{-1} + T^T(T\Omega_k T^T + \Sigma)^{-1}](Tb)$$

yields. This leads to the result

(149) $$2a_{k,N}(z) = a^T Fa + [Tb - E^{-1}((T\Omega_k T^T + \Sigma)^{-1}T + d_N\Sigma^{-1}T\bar{\Omega}_M\Omega_k^{-1})a]^T$$

$$E[Tb - E^{-1}((T\Omega_k T^T + \Sigma)^{-1}T + d_N\Sigma^{-1}T\bar{\Omega}_M\Omega_k^{-1})a]$$

with

(150) $$E := d_N^2\Sigma^{-1}T\bar{\Omega}_M\Omega_k^{-1}\bar{\Omega}_M T^T\Sigma^{-1} + (T\Omega_k T^T + \Sigma)^{-1}$$

$$= (d_N T\Omega_M T^T + \Sigma)^{-1}T\, d_N^2\,\Omega_M\Omega_k^{-1}\Omega_M T^T(d_N T\Omega_M T^T + \Sigma)^{-1} + (T\Omega_k T^T + \Sigma)^{-1} \qquad \text{(see (141))}$$

(151) $$F := \Omega_k^{-1} + T^T(T\Omega_k T^T+\Sigma)^{-1}T -$$

$$[d_N\Omega_k^{-1}\bar{\Omega}_M T^T\Sigma^{-1} + T^T(T\Omega_k T^T+\Sigma)^{-1}]E^{-1}[d_N\Sigma^{-1}T\bar{\Omega}_M\Omega_k^{-1} + (T\Omega_k T^T+\Sigma)^{-1}T]$$

According to (150), E is positive definite (see (163)) and because of

$$Tb = z - T(\mu_M - \alpha_M\Omega_M 1\!\!1)$$

it immediately follows from (128),(149):

(152) $$A(k,N) = \frac{1}{2\alpha_k}\ln|(T\Omega_k T^T+\Sigma)E| + \frac{1}{2\alpha_k}a^T Fa$$

For F, this yields (see (141),(151)):

(153) $$F = \Omega_k^{-1} + T^T(T\Omega_k T^T+\Sigma)^{-1}T - [d_N\Omega_k^{-1}\Omega_M T^T(d_N T\Omega_M T^T+\Sigma)^{-1}$$

$$+ T^T(T\Omega_k T^T+\Sigma)^{-1}]E^{-1}[d_N(d_N T\Omega_M T^T+\Sigma)^{-1}T\Omega_M\Omega_k^{-1} + (T\Omega_k T^T+\Sigma)^{-1}T]$$

It holds (see (150)):

$$d_N(d_N T\Omega_M T^T+\Sigma)^{-1}T\Omega_M\Omega_k^{-1} + (T\Omega_k T^T+\Sigma)^{-1}T =$$

$$ET + d_N(d_N T\Omega_M T^T+\Sigma)^{-1}T\Omega_M\Omega_k^{-1}(Id_n - d_N\Omega_M T^T(d_N T\Omega_M T^T+\Sigma)^{-1}T)$$

and (see (167)):

(154) $$Id_n - d_N\Omega_M T^T(d_N T\Omega_M T^T+\Sigma)^{-1}T = (\Omega_M^{-1} + d_N T^T\Sigma^{-1}T)^{-1}\Omega_M^{-1}$$

which yields for (153):

(155) $$F = \Omega_k^{-1} + T^T(T\Omega_k T^T+\Sigma)^{-1}T - [d_N\Omega_k^{-1}\Omega_M T^T(d_N T\Omega_M T^T+\Sigma)^{-1} + T^T(T\Omega_k T^T+\Sigma)^{-1}]T$$

$$- d_N T^T(d_N T\Omega_M T^T+\Sigma)^{-1}T\Omega_M\Omega_k^{-1} + T^T(d_N T\Omega_M T^T+\Sigma)^{-1}Td_N^2\Omega_M\Omega_k^{-1}\Omega_M T^T(d_N T\Omega_M T^T+\Sigma)^{-1}T$$

$$- \Omega_M^{-1}(\Omega_M^{-1} + d_N T^T\Sigma^{-1}T)^{-1}\Omega_k^{-1}\Omega_M T^T$$

$$[T\Omega_M\Omega_k^{-1}\Omega_M T^T + d_N^{-2}(d_N T\Omega_M T^T+\Sigma)(T\Omega_k T^T+\Sigma)^{-1}(d_N T\Omega_M T^T+\Sigma)]^{-1}$$

$$T\Omega_M\Omega_k^{-1}(\Omega_M^{-1} + d_N T^T\Sigma^{-1}T)^{-1}\Omega_M^{-1}$$

According to (154)

$$\Omega_k^{-1}-d_N\Omega_k^{-1}\Omega_M T^T(d_N T\Omega_M T^T+\Sigma)^{-1}T-d_N T(d_N T\Omega_M T^T+\Sigma)^{-1}T\Omega_M\Omega_k^{-1}$$

$$+ T^T(d_N T\Omega_M T^T+\Sigma)^{-1}Td_N^2\Omega_M\Omega_k^{-1}\Omega_M T^T(d_N T\Omega_M T^T+\Sigma)^{-1}T$$

$$= \Omega_k^{-1}(\Omega_M^{-1}+d_N T^T\Sigma^{-1}T)^{-1}\Omega_M^{-1}$$

$$- d_N T^T(d_N T\Omega_M T^T+\Sigma)^{-1}T\Omega_M\Omega_k^{-1}(\Omega_M^{-1}+d_N T^T\Sigma^{-1}T)^{-1}\Omega_M^{-1}$$

$$= \Omega_M^{-1}(\Omega_M^{-1}+d_N T^T\Sigma^{-1}T)^{-1}\Omega_k^{-1}(\Omega_M^{-1}+d_N T^T\Sigma^{-1}T)^{-1}\Omega_M^{-1}$$

For (155), this yields (see (141),(167)):

$$F = \Omega_M^{-1}(\Omega_M^{-1}+d_N T^T\Sigma^{-1}T)^{-1}\Omega_k^{-1}\Omega_M[\Omega_M\Omega_k^{-1}\Omega_M -$$

$$T^T(T\Omega_M\Omega_k^{-1}\Omega_M T^T+d_N^{-2}(d_N T\Omega_M T^T+\Sigma)(T\Omega_k T^T+\Sigma)^{-1}(d_N T\Omega_M T^T+\Sigma))^{-1}T]$$

$$\Omega_M\Omega_k^{-1}(\Omega_M^{-1}+d_N T^T\Sigma^{-1}T)^{-1}\Omega_M^{-1}$$

$$= \Omega_M^{-1}(\Omega_M^{-1}+d_N T^T\Sigma^{-1}T)^{-1}\Omega_k^{-1}\Omega_M[\Omega_M^{-1}\Omega_k\Omega_M^{-1}$$

$$(\Omega_M^{-1}\Omega_k\Omega_M^{-1}+d_N^2T^T(d_N T\Omega_M T^T+\Sigma)^{-1}(T\Omega_k T^T+\Sigma)(d_N T\Omega_M T^T+\Sigma)^{-1}T)^{-1}$$

$$\Omega_M^{-1}\Omega_k\Omega_M^{-1}]\Omega_M\Omega_k^{-1}(\Omega_M^{-1}+d_N T^T\Sigma^{-1}T)^{-1}\Omega_M^{-1}$$

$$= \Omega_M^{-1}[(\Omega_M^{-1}+d_N T^T\Sigma^{-1}T)\Omega_k(\Omega_M^{-1}+d_N T^T\Sigma^{-1}T)$$

$$+ d_N^2T^T\Sigma^{-1}(T\Omega_k T^T+\Sigma)\Sigma^{-1}T]^{-1}\Omega_M^{-1}$$

and (126) follows from (152).

Finally, (127) is shown:

From (148), it follows

$$2b_{k,N}(z) = 2a_{k,N}(z) - 2a^T\Omega_k^{-1}(a-d_N\bar{\Omega}_M T^T\Sigma^{-1}Tb) + 2a^T\Omega_k^{-1}\mu_k$$

$$= a^TT^T(T\Omega_k T^T+\Sigma)^{-1}Ta + a^T\Omega_k^{-1}(2\mu_k-a)+(Tb)^T E\,Tb-2a^TT^T(T\Omega_k T^T+\Sigma)^{-1}Tb$$

$$= (Tb-E^{-1}(T\Omega_k T^T+\Sigma)^{-1}Ta)^T E(Tb-E^{-1}(T\Omega_k T^T+\Sigma)^{-1}Ta)$$

$$+ a^T[T^T(T\Omega_k T^T+\Sigma)^{-1}T-T^T(T\Omega_k T^T+\Sigma)^{-1}E^{-1}(T\Omega_k T^T+\Sigma)^{-1}T]a+a^T\Omega_k^{-1}(2\mu_k-a)$$

By this, it directly follows from (123),(129):

$$B(k,N) = \frac{1}{2\alpha_k} \ell n \,|(T\Omega_k T^T+\Sigma)E|$$

$$+ \frac{1}{2\alpha_k} a^T T^T [(T\Omega_k T^T+\Sigma)^{-1} - (T\Omega_k T^T+\Sigma)^{-1}E^{-1}(T\Omega_k T^T+\Sigma)^{-1}]Ta + B(k,\emptyset)$$

and (127) follows from (see (150)):

$$(T\Omega_k T^T+\Sigma)^{-1} - (T\Omega_k T^T+\Sigma)^{-1}E^{-1}(T\Omega_k T^T+\Sigma)^{-1}$$

$$= (T\Omega_k T^T+\Sigma)^{-1}E^{-1}(E-(T\Omega_k T^T+\Sigma)^{-1})$$

$$= (T\Omega_k T^T+\Sigma)^{-1}E^{-1}[(d_N T\Omega_M T^T+\Sigma)^{-1}Td_N^2\Omega_M\Omega_k^{-1}\Omega_M T^T(d_N T\Omega_M T^T+\Sigma)^{-1}]$$

$$= [T\Omega_k T^T+\Sigma+(d_N T\Omega_M T^T+\Sigma)(Td_N^2\Omega_M\Omega_k^{-1}\Omega_M T^T)^{-1}(d_N T\Omega_M T^T+\Sigma)]^{-1} \qquad \square$$

According to (115),(116) or (119),(120), respectively, theorem 11 allows for the information systems described in theorem 3 hence, for normally distributed,unbiased estimators of arbitrarily linear transformed prices to explicitly determine EVI and ETVI.[1]

Theorem 11 also admits some conclusions generally valid for this class of information systems:

- If $a=0$, i.e. if $\mu_k = \mu_M - \alpha_M\Omega_M 1\!\!1$, then always (i.e. $\forall\, N \subset M$, $\forall\, k \in M$)

  $$EVI(k,N) = ETVI(k,N) .$$

  This is not astonishing, for according to (84) the condition $a=0$ is equivalent to the condition $y_k^* = 0$, i.e. the prior optimal portfolio is risk free.

- Let $k \in N$. It holds (see (115),(116),(122),(124),(125)):

(156) $$ETVI(k,N) = \frac{1}{2\alpha_k} \ell n \frac{|T\Omega_k T^T+\Sigma|\,|d_N^2 T\Omega_M\Omega_k^{-1}\Omega_M T^T+\Sigma|}{|d_N T\Omega_M T^T+\Sigma|^2}$$

(157) $$EVI(k,N) = ETVI(k,N) - \frac{1}{2\alpha_k} a^T[\Omega_k^{-1} - (\Omega_k + d_N^2\Omega_M T^T\Sigma^{-1}T\Omega_M)^{-1}]a$$

---

1) Besides knowing his individual prior data $\mu_k, \Omega_k, \alpha_k$ and the data T, Σ of the information system, however, the investor needs to know the market data $\mu_M, \Omega_M, \alpha_M$ and the portion d_N of informed investors.

As

$$\Omega_k^{-1} - (\Omega_k + d_N^2 \Omega_M T^T \Sigma^{-1} T \Omega_M)^{-1}$$

$$= \Omega_M^{-1} [\Omega_M \Omega_k^{-1} \Omega_M - ((\Omega_M \Omega_k^{-1} \Omega_M)^{-1} + T^T d_N^2 \Sigma^{-1} T)^{-1}] \Omega_M^{-1}$$

$$= \Omega_M^{-1} [\Omega_M \Omega_k^{-1} \Omega_M + \Omega_M \Omega_k^{-1} \Omega_M T^T (T\Omega_M \Omega_k^{-1} \Omega_M T^T + d_N^{-2} \Sigma)^{-1} T \Omega_M \Omega_k^{-1} \Omega_M - \Omega_M \Omega_k^{-1} \Omega_M] \Omega_M^{-1}$$

(see (167))

$$= \Omega_k^{-1} \Omega_M T^T (T\Omega_M \Omega_k^{-1} \Omega_M T^T + d_N^{-2} \Sigma)^{-1} T \Omega_M \Omega_k^{-1}$$

is positive semidefinite, it holds for $k \in N$:

$$\text{EVI}(k,N) \leq \text{ETVI}(k,N) \; .$$

If one looks on d_N as a continuous variable which can be justified for big markets, then it follows from (156),(157) for $k \in N$:

$$\lim_{d_N \to 0} \text{ETVI}(k,N) = \lim_{d_N \to 0} \text{EVI}(k,N) = \frac{1}{2\alpha_k} \ln \frac{|T\Omega_k T^T + \Sigma|}{|\Sigma|}$$

which is equivalent to the result (55) in theorem 5.

If the group of informed investors is sufficiently small, hence, the resultsderived in Sec. 2 yield.

In the case of prior homogeneous covariances for $M = N$ according to (156),(157) because of $d_M = 1$, and $\Omega_k = \Omega_M = \Omega$:

(158) $$\text{ETVI}(k,M) = 0$$

(159) $$\text{EVI}(k,M) = -\frac{1}{2\alpha_k} a^T T^T (T\Omega T^T + \Sigma)^{-1} T a \leq 0$$

hold.

If $Ta \neq 0$, in (159) the strong inequality holds.[1]

According to (156), in the case of prior homogeneous covariances

(160) $$\lim_{\Sigma \to 0} \text{ETVI}(k,N) = 0$$

for any N with $k \in N$, therefore also especially for $N = \{k\}$. Hence, perfect insider information has - as each perfect information - the total information value zero. This result shows the distance from reality of the hybrid model at perfect or approximatively perfect

1) Also Wahl [1983] shows for logarithmic utility functions that published information do not have a positive value for the case of homogeneous expectations.

information levels which as mentioned above, however, are meaningless for realistic considerations. The explanation for result (160) is that a perfectly informed investor within the framework of the hybrid model - as it is presupposed here - does not speculate against the market, but directly causes by his changed demand behavior such equilibrium prices which secure the rate of return r for each asset. However, this does not improve - as presented in example 5 - his decision situation.

• Let $k \notin N$. As mentioned then the information values can not be pragmatically interpreted. According to (121)

$$\mathrm{ETVI}(k,M) \geq 0$$ [1]

where the advantage of such an information activity is only fictitious and is explained by the unchanged information level obsolete in comparison to the information level of the informed investors. If d_N is small, i.e. if the equilibrium prices are only changed very little by the information activity, then also the effect for the investor k is very small $(k \notin N)$:

(161) $$\lim_{d_N \to 0} \mathrm{ETVI}(k,N) = \lim_{d_N \to 0} \mathrm{EVI}(k,N) = 0$$

(161) immediately follows from (122),(126),(127).

Particularly clear results yield, if only one risky asset is considered:

Example 6:

Let especially be $n=1$. Thus $t=1$ and without loss of generality T is the identity matrix: $T=(1)$. With

$$\Omega_k =: (\omega_k^2)$$

$$\Omega_M =: (\omega_M^2)$$

$$\Sigma =: (\sigma^2)$$

for $k \in N$ according to (156),(157) results

$$\mathfrak{f}(d_N) := \mathrm{ETVI}(k,N) = \frac{1}{2\alpha_k} \ln \frac{(\omega_k^2+\sigma^2)\left(d_N^2 \frac{\omega_M^4}{\omega_k^2} + \sigma^2\right)}{(d_N\omega_M^2 + \sigma^2)^2}$$

[1] From (127), even the strong inequality holds.

If d_N is interpreted as a continuous, positive variable and if the limitation $d_N \leq 1$ is firstly not considered, then for f the following properties result

- $f(d_N) \geq 0 \quad \forall\, d_N \geq 0$ (see (121))

- $f(0) = \frac{1}{2\alpha_k} \ln \frac{\omega_k^2 + \sigma^2}{\sigma^2}$

- $f(+\infty) := \lim\limits_{d_N \to +\infty} f(d_N) = \frac{1}{2\alpha_k} \ln \frac{\omega_k^2 + \sigma^2}{\omega_k^2}$

  Normally, $\sigma^2 > \omega_k^2$ can be assumed, i.e. $f(0) < f(+\infty)$.

- $f(0) < f(1) \Leftrightarrow \omega_k^2 < \omega_M^2 \frac{1}{2 + \frac{\omega_M^2}{\sigma^2}}$

  If realistically $\sigma^2 > \omega_M^2$, then a published information $(d_N = 1)$ is for investor k in any case better than insider information $(d_N \approx 0)$, if $\omega_k^2 < \omega_M^2 / 3$. Prior very well informed investors are rather interested in publishing the information.

- f is minimal for $d_N^* = \frac{\omega_k^2}{\omega_M^2}$, and

  $f(d_N^*) = 0$. Depending on whether ω_k^2 is greater than ω_M^2 (f_1) . equal to ω_M^2 (f_2) or smaller than ω_M^2 (f_3) , three characteristic cases result (assumed that the variables α_k, σ^2 and ω_M^2 are fixed):

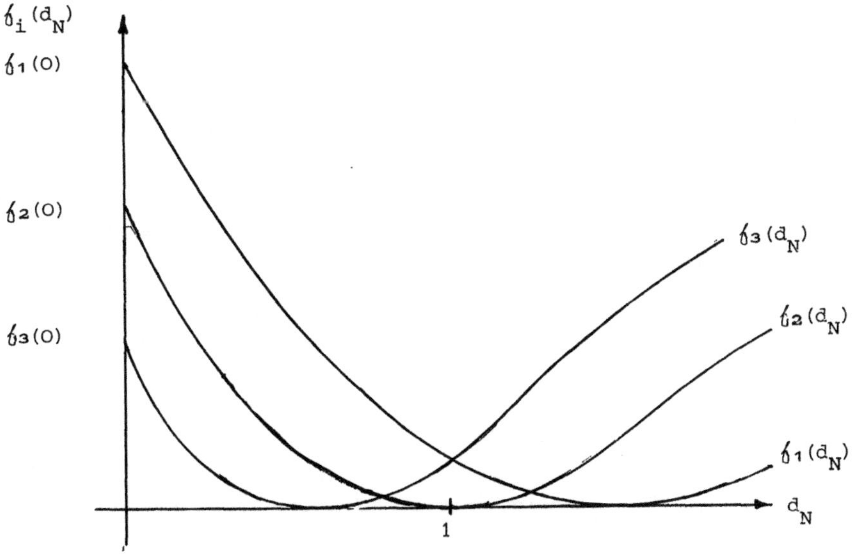

If ETVI(k,N) is considered as a function of σ^2 with fixed other variables, then the ETVI(k,N) is maximal for $\sigma^2 = d_N\omega_M^2$. Hence, there is an optimal estimation precision for all informed investors.[1]

The EVI(k,N) is always not greater than the ETVI(k,N) :

$$\mathrm{EVI}(k,N) = \mathrm{ETVI}(k,N) - \frac{a^2\, d_N^2\, \omega_M^4}{\omega_k^2(\omega_M^4 d_N^2 + \sigma^2\omega_k^2)} =: g(d_N)$$

where the difference depends on $a = \mu_k - \mu_M + \alpha_M\omega_M^2$ $(\in \mathbb{R})$. The difference $f(d_N) - g(d_N)$ is monotonously increasing and bounded. The following figure illustrates this relation for $a \neq 0$ (assumed that all other variables are fixed):

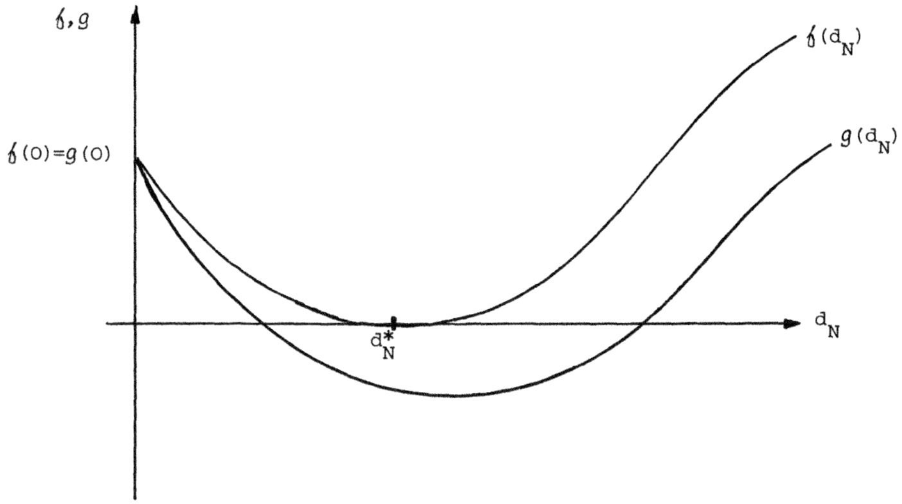

Also for $k \notin N$, the situation can easily be analyzed for the case $n = 1$. In particular, it shows that ETVI(k,N) is monotonously increasing as function of d_N . This is explained from the price changes which are more extensive with increasing d_N and which are favourably evaluated by an uninformed investor within the scope of his obsolete information level.

1) For $\sigma^2 = 0$ or $\sigma^2 \to \infty$ the information value zero results, see (160).

4. Appendix

Some technical statements follow which were referred to in the text. According to the personal preknowledge, the compilation may appear more or less arbitrary.

(162) Let $a,b,c \in \mathbb{R}^n$, $A,B, \in \mathbb{R}^{(n,n)}$ be symmetric and $A+B$ be nonsingular. Then

$$(a-b)^T A(a-b) + (c-b)^T B(c-b) =$$
$$((A+B)^{-1}(Aa+Bc)-b)^T (A+B)((A+B)^{-1}(Aa+Bc)-b) + (c-a)^T B(A+B)^{-1} A(c-a)$$

Proof:

(see Raiffa, Schlaifer [1961])

Obviously,

$$(a-b)^T A(a-b) + (c-b)^T B(c-b)$$
$$= b^T(A+B)b - 2b^T(Aa+Bc) + a^T Aa + c^T Bc$$
$$= ((A+B)^{-1}(Aa+Bc)-b)^T (A+B)((A+B)^{-1}(Aa+Bc)-b)$$
$$- (Aa+Bc)^T (A+B)^{-1}(Aa+Bc) + a^T Aa + c^T Bc$$

Further

$$(Aa+Bc)^T (A+B)^{-1}(Aa+Bc)$$
$$= ((A+B)a + B(c-a))^T (A+B)^{-1}(A(a-c) + (A+B)c)$$
$$= a^T A(a-c) + a^T (A+B)c + (c-a)^T B(A+B)^{-1}A(a-c)$$
$$+ (c-a)^T Bc = a^T Aa + c^T Bc - (c-a)^T B(A+B)^{-1}A(c-a) .$$ □

Positive (semi)definite matrices are always assumed to be symmetric.

(163) Let $A,B \in \mathbb{R}^{(n,n)}$, A be positive definite and B be positive semidefinite. Then $A+B$ is positive definite.

Proof:

Let $x \in \mathbb{R}^n$, $x \neq 0$, then $x^T Ax > 0$, $x^T Bx \geq 0$ and with this $x^T(A+B)x > x^T Bx \geq 0$. Furthermore, $A+B$ is symmetric. □

(164) Let $A,B \in \mathbb{R}^{(n,n)}$ be positive definite and $a,b \in \mathbb{R}$; $a,b \geq 0$; $a+b > 0$, then $aA + bB$ is positive definite.

The proof follows from (163), because aA, bB are positive semidefinite and at least one of these two matrices is positive definite. It immediately follows

(165) Convex combinations of positive definite matrices are positive definite.

(166) Let $A \in \mathbb{R}^{(n,n)}$ be positive semidefinite. Then $f : \mathbb{R}^n \to \mathbb{R}$, $f(y) := y^T Ay$ is convex. If A is positive definite, then f is strictly convex.

Proof:

Let $\lambda \in [0,1]$; $x, y \in \mathbb{R}^n$, then

$$\lambda x^T Ax + (1-\lambda)y^T Ay - (\lambda x + (1-\lambda)y)^T A(\lambda x + (1-\lambda)y)$$

$$= (\lambda-\lambda^2)x^T Ax + ((1-\lambda) - (1-\lambda)^2)y^T Ay - 2\lambda(1-\lambda)[x^T Ay]$$

$$= \lambda(1-\lambda)(x-y)^T A(x-y) \geq 0$$

and the strict inequality holds if $\lambda \in (0,1)$, $x \neq y$ and A is positive definite. □

(167) Let $A \in \mathbb{R}^{(n,n)}$, $B \in \mathbb{R}^{(u,u)}$ be positive definite matrices and $U \in \mathbb{R}^{(u,n)}$ with $\text{rank}(U) = u$, then

a) $(UAU^T+B)^{-1} = B^{-1}(B - U(A^{-1} + U^T B^{-1}U)^{-1}U^T)B^{-1}$

b) $U^T(UAU^T + B)^{-1}U = A^{-1}(A^{-1} + U^T B^{-1}U)^{-1}U^T B^{-1}U$

Proof:

A and B are positive definite therefore, all inverse matrices occuring in the following exist. The statement (167) could also be proved under a little weaker assumptions. It holds

$$UAU^T = UA(U^T B^{-1}U+A^{-1})(A^{-1}+U^T B^{-1}U)^{-1}U^T$$

$$= (UAU^T+B)B^{-1}U(A^{-1}+U^T B^{-1}U)^{-1}U^T$$

and with this

$$B^{-1} - (UAU^T+B)^{-1} = (UAU^T+B)^{-1}UAU^T B^{-1}$$

$$= B^{-1}U(A^{-1}+U^T B^{-1}U)^{-1}U^T B^{-1}$$

which shows a). The statement b) then immediately follows:

$$U^T B^{-1}U-U^T(UAU^T+B)^{-1}U$$

$$= (U^T B^{-1}U+A^{-1}-A^{-1})(A^{-1}+U^T B^{-1}U)^{-1}U^T B^{-1}U$$

$$= U^T B^{-1}U-A^{-1}(A^{-1}+U^T B^{-1}U)^{-1}U^T B^{-1}U \; .$$ □

(168) Let $A \in \mathbb{R}^{(n,m)}$, $B \in \mathbb{R}^{(m,n)}$, then

$$|AB + Id_n| = |BA + Id_m|$$

Proof:

(see e.g. Dhrymes [1978], p. 457)

$$\left|\begin{pmatrix} AB+Id_n & A \\ O & Id_m \end{pmatrix}\right| = \left|\begin{pmatrix} Id_n & A \\ -B & Id_m \end{pmatrix}\begin{pmatrix} Id_n & O \\ B & Id_m \end{pmatrix}\right|$$

$$\left|\begin{pmatrix} Id_n & O \\ B & Id_m \end{pmatrix}\begin{pmatrix} Id_n & A \\ -B & Id_m \end{pmatrix}\right| = \left|\begin{pmatrix} Id_n & A \\ O & BA+Id_m \end{pmatrix}\right|$$ □

(169) Let $A,B \in \mathbb{R}^{(n,n)}$ be positive definite and $B \gtrsim A$, i.e. $B-A$ positive semidefinite, then

$$|B| \geq |A|$$

where the equality only holds, if $A = B$.

For the proof see e.g. Dhrymes [1978], p. 495 f.

(170) Let $A,B \in \mathbb{R}^{(n,n)}$ be positive definite matrices and $U \in \mathbb{R}^{(u,n)}$ with $\text{rank}(U) = u$, then

$$\frac{|A+B|}{|B|} \geq \frac{|U(A+B)U^T|}{|UBU^T|} > 1$$

where the equality only holds for the case $u = n$.

Proof:

If $u = n$, U is invertible, and obviously the equality holds.

Let $u < n$. First it is shown that

$$D := B^{-1} - U^T(UBU^T)^{-1}U$$

is positive semidefinite and unequal to the null matrix. $(UBU^T)^{-1}$ is positive definite, therefore

$$\text{rank}(U^T (UBU^T)^{-1}U) = u < n = \text{rank}(B^{-1}),$$

i.e. $D \neq O$. Furthermore, D is symmetric.

Let λ be an eigenvalue of D for the eigenvector $x \neq O$:

$$\lambda x = B^{-1}x - U^T(UBU^T)^{-1}Ux$$

$$\Rightarrow \lambda UBx = Ux - Ux = O$$

If $\lambda \neq O$, thus $UBx = O$, and

$$\lambda x^T Bx = x^T x - x^T BU^T (UBU^T)^{-1}Ux = x^T x$$

or

$$\lambda = \frac{x^T x}{x^T Bx} > 0$$

Thus, D does not have negative eigenvalues, i.e. D is positive semidefinite.

As A is positive definite, an invertible matrix $C \in \mathbb{R}^{(n,n)}$ exists with $A = C^T C$.

The matrices

$$E := Id_n + CB^{-1}C^T$$

$$F := Id_n + CU^T(UBU^T)^{-1}UC^T$$

are positive definite and $E - F = \underline{C}DC^T$ is - as shown above - positive semidefinite and unequal to the null matrix. Hence (see (169)):

$$|E| > |F|$$

Finally, it follows from (168)

$$|E| = |Id_n + C^T CB^{-1}| = \frac{|A+B|}{|B|}$$

$$|F| = |Id_u + (UBU^T)^{-1}UC^T CU^T| = \frac{|U(A+B)U^T|}{|UBU^T|}$$

The second inequality in (170) immediately follows from (169), because

$$U(A+B)U^T, \; UBU^T \text{ and } U(A+B)U^T - UBU^T = UAU^T$$

are positive definite. □

(171) Let $A, \Omega \in \mathbb{R}^{(n,n)}$, $\mu \in \mathbb{R}^n$, Ω be positive semidefinite and $X = (X_1, \ldots, X_n)^T$ be an n-dimensional random variable with $EX = \mu$, $\mathrm{Cov}X = \Omega$, then

$$E(X^T AX) = \mu^T A\mu + Sp(A\Omega)$$

Proof:

With the notations $\mu = (\mu_1, \ldots, \mu_n)^T$, $A = (a_{ij})$, $\Omega = (\omega_{ij})$ it holds

$$E(X^T AX) = \sum_{i,j} a_{ij} E(X_i X_j)$$

$$= \sum_{i,j} a_{ij}(\omega_{ij} + \mu_i \mu_j)$$

$$\sum_{i,j} \mu_i a_{ij} \mu_i + \sum_i (\sum_j a_{ij} \omega_{ji})$$

□

(172) Let $C \in \mathbb{R}^{(t,t)}$, $c_1 \in \mathbb{R}^t$, $c_0 \in \mathbb{R}$ anc C be positive definite, then it holds

$$\int_{-\infty}^{+\infty} \exp\{-(z^T \frac{C}{2} z - z^T c_1 + \frac{c_0}{2})\} dz$$

$$= (2\pi)^{t/2} |C|^{-1/2} \exp\{\frac{1}{2}(c_1^T C^{-1} c_1 - c_0)\}$$

Regarding the proof see e.g. Graybill [1969], p. 252.

For the last three statements, let always $A \subset \mathbb{R}^n$, $B \subset \mathbb{R}^m$ and

$f : A \times B \to \mathbb{R}$.

(173) Let A, B be non-empty, closed, convex and f concave-convex.[1] If A or B is bounded, it holds

$$\inf_{y \in B} \sup_{x \in A} f(x,y) = \sup_{x \in A} \inf_{y \in B} f(x,y)$$

Regarding the proof see e.g. Rockafellar [1970], Sec. 37.3.2, p. 393.

(174) Let $A' \subset A$

If[2]

$$\max_{x \in A'} f(x,y) = \max_{x \in A} f(x,y) \quad \forall\ y \in B$$

and

(*) $$\min_{y \in B} \max_{x \in A'} f(x,y) = \max_{x \in A'} \min_{y \in B} f(x,y) =: v$$

then it holds (in particular, the following extrema exist)

(**) $$\min_{y \in B} \max_{x \in A} f(x,y) = \max_{x \in A} \min_{y \in B} f(x,y) = v$$

and each equilibrium point of (*) is also such a point of (**).

Proof:

$$\max_{x \in A'} \min_{y \in B} f(x,y) \le \sup_{x \in A} \min_{y \in B} f(x,y)$$

$$\le \inf_{y \in B} \sup_{x \in A} f(x,y) = \inf_{y \in B} \max_{x \in A} f(x,y)$$

$$= \inf_{y \in B} \max_{x \in A'} f(x,y) = \max_{x \in A'} \min_{y \in B} f(x,y) ,$$

---

[1] i.e. f is concave in the first and convex in the second argument with in each case fixed other argument.

[2] In particular, all extrema may exist.

i.e. the equality always holds, and the extrema are attained. Then the last statement is evident, for:

Let $y^* \in B$ be an equilibrium strategy of $(*) \Rightarrow$

$$\max_{x \in A'} f(x,y^*) = v \Rightarrow \max_{x \in A} f(x,y^*) = v ,$$

i.e. y^* is also an equilibrium strategy of $(**)$.

Let $x^* \in A$ be an equilibrium strategy of $(*) \Rightarrow$

$\min_{y \in B} f(x^*,y) = v$ **and** x^* is because of

$A' \subset A$, i.e. $x^* \in A$,

also an equilibrium strategy of $(**)$. □

(175) Let A,B be compact[1] and f continuous, then

$$g : A \to \mathbb{R}$$

$$g(x) := \min_{y \in B} f(x,y)$$

is continuous.

<u>Proof:</u>

Let $x_0 \in A$, $\varepsilon > 0$. As f is uniformly continuous on $A \times B$, a $\delta > 0$ exists such that

$$\forall\, y \in B ,\ x \in A :$$
$$\|x - x_0\| < \delta \Rightarrow |f(x_0,y) - f(x,y)| < \varepsilon$$

Let $x' \in A$, $\|x' - x_0\| < \delta$ and $y_0, y' \in B$ with

$$g(x_0) = f(x_0,y_0)$$
$$g(x') = f(x',y')$$

then it holds

$$g(x') = \min_{y \in B} f(x',y) \le f(x',y_0) < f(x_0,x_0) + \varepsilon = g(x_0) + \varepsilon$$

$$g(x') = f(x',y') > f(x^0,y') - \varepsilon \ge \min_{y \in B} f(x^0,y) - \varepsilon = g(x_0) - \varepsilon$$

i.e. $|g(x') - g(x_0)| < \varepsilon$ □

---

[1] The compactness requirement of A can be weakened.

Index

References

Ackoff, R.L. [1968]: Towards a Behavioral Theory of Communication Management Science, 4, 3, 218-234

Albach, H. [1961]: Entscheidungsprozeß und Informationsfluß in der Unternehmensorganisation, in: Organisation. TFB-Handbuchreihe, 1. Bd., ed. by E. Schnaufer and Aghte, 355-402

Albach, H. [1969]: Informationswert, in E. Grochla (Ed.) Handwörterbuch der Organisation, Stuttgart, 720-727

Amihud, Y. [1980]: General Risk Aversion and Attitude Towards Risk, Journal of Finance 35, 685-691

Andersen, T.M. [1983]: Price and Quantity Signals in Financial Markets, Zeitschrift für Nationalökonomie 43, 109-129

Arrow, K.J. [1965]: The Theory of Risk Aversion, Reprinted and Appendix Added in: Arrow (1970) Essays in the Theory of Risk-Bearing, 90-120

Arrow, K.J. [1972]: The Value of and Demand for Information, C.B. McGuire and R. Radner (Ed.): Decision and Organisation, North-Holland Publishing Company, Amsterdam-London

Bamberg, G. [1974]: Der Minimax-Wert der Stichprobeninformation, Operations Research Verfahren XXI, VII. Oberwolfach-Tagung über OR, 14-23

Bamberg, G. [1975]: Wieviel dürfen Informationen kosten? in: Bamberg, G.; Opitz, O. (Ed.): Information und Prognose, Meisenheim

Bamberg, G. [1983]: The Hybrid Model and Related Approaches to Capital Market Equilibria, Arbeitspapiere zur Mathematischen Wirtschaftsforschung, Heft 61, Universität Augsburg

Bamberg, G.; Coenenberg, A.G.; Kleine-Doepke, R. [1976]: Zur entscheidungsorientierten Bewertung von Informationen, Zeitschrift für betriebswirtschaftliche Forschung, 1, 28, 30-42

Bamberg, G.; Firchau, V. [1981]: Some Remarks on the Aggregation Theorem for Divergent Borrowing and Lending Rates, Methods of Operations Research, 44, 465-476

Bamberg, G.; Spremann, K. [1981]: Implications of Constant Risk Aversion, Zeitschrift für Operations Research, 25, 205-224

Bamberg, G.; Spremann, K. [1983]: Risikoprämien und Informationswerte bei lokaler Konsistenz, in: Mathematische Systeme in der Ökonomie (Ed. M.J. Beckmann, W. Eichhorn, W. Krelle), Athenäum, 77-100

Baron, D.P. [1974]: Information, Investment Behavior, and Efficient Portfolios, Journal of Financial and Quantitative Analysis 9, 555-566

Barry, C.B. [1974]: Portfolio Analysis under Uncertain Means, Variances, and Covariances, Journal of Finance 29, 515-522

Bawa, V.S. [1982]: Stochastic Dominance: A Research Bibliography, Management Science 28, 698-712

Bawa, V.S.; Brown, S.J.; Klein, R.W. [1979]: Estimation Risk and Optimal Portfolio Choice, North-Holland Publishing Company, Amsterdam-New York-Oxford

Bawa, V.S.; Goroff, D.L. [1983]: Stochastic Dominance, Efficiency and Separation in Finanancial Markets, Journal of Economic Theory 30, 410-414

Behara, M. [1974]: Entropy and Utility, G. Menges (Ed.): Information, Inference and Decision, Theory and Decision Library, D. Reidel Publishing Company, Dordrecht-Holland-Boston, 145-154

Behara, M.; Kofler, E.; Menges, G. [1978]: Entropy and Informativity in Decision Situations under Partial Information, Statistische Hefte 2, 124-130

Bernardo, J.M. [1979]: Expected Information as Expected Utility, The Annals of Staitistics 7, 3, 686-690

Bierlein, D. [1963]: Einheitliche Prinzipien für die Beurteilung statistischer Verfahren, Blätter der Deutschen Gesellschaft für Versicherungsmathematik 6, 442-456

Bitz, M. [1975]: Modelle zur Informationsbewertung, Zeitschrift für Betriebswirtschaft 9, 45, 521-546

Bitz, M. [1981]: Entscheidungstheorie, Verlag Franz Vahlen, München

Blau, R.A. [1974]: Stochastic Programming and Decision Analysis: An Apparent Dilemma, Management Science 21, 3, 271-276

Blog, B.; Van der Hoek, G.; Rinnooy Kan, A.H.G.; Timmer, G.T. [1983]: The Optimal Selection of Small Portfolios, Management Science 29, 792-798

Brennan, M.J. [1971]: Capital Market Equilibrium with Divergent Borrowing and Lending Rates, Journal of Financial and Quantitative Analysis 6, 1197-1205

Brennan, M.J. [1975]: The Optimal Number of Securities in a Risky Asset Portfolio when there are Fixed Costs of Transacting: Theory and Some Results, Journal of Financial and Quantitative Analysis 10, 483-496

Buchner, R. [1982]: Das Separationstheorem von Tobin, WiST, 6-14

Bühler, W. [1977]: Portefeuilleplanung bei unvollkommen bekannten Mittwelwerten und Varianzen, Proceedings in Operations Research 7, 158-167

Bühler, W. [1984]: Capital Budgeting and Financial Planning under Qualitative Data Information, in J.P. Brans (Ed.): Operational Research '84 (preprints), Part II, 947-962

Burger, E. [1966]: Einführung in die Theorie der Spiele, 2. Auflage, Walter de Gruyter, Berlin

Cass, D.; Stiglitz, J.E. [1970]: The Structure of Investor Preferences and Asset Returns, and Separability in Portfolio Allocation, Journal of Economic Theory 2, 122-160

Chamberlain [1983]: A Characterization of the Distributions that Imply Mean-Variance Utility Functions, Journal of Economic Theory 29, 185-201

Cohen, K.J.; Hawawini, G.A.; Maier, S.F.; Schwartz, R.A.; Whitcomb, D.K. [1983]: Estimating and Adjusting for the Intervalling-Effect Bias in Beta, Management Science 29, 135-147

Colson, G.; Zeleny, M. [1980]: Uncertain Prospects Ranking and Portfolio Analysis under the Conditions of Partial Information, Verlag A. Hain, Meisenheim

Cooper, M.W.; Farhangian, K. [1982]: An Integer Programming Algorithm for Portfolio Selection with Fixed Charges, Naval Research Logistics Quarterly 29, 147-150

Copeland, T.E. [1976]: A Model of Asset Trading under the Assumption of Sequential Information Arrival, Journal of Finance 31, 1149-1168

DeGroot, M.H. [1962]: Uncertainty, Information, and Sequential Experiments, Ann. Math. Statist. 33, 404-419

Dhrymes, P.J. [1978]: Introductory Econometrics, Springer-Verlag, Berlin-Heidelberg-New York

Diamond, D.W.; Verreccia, R.E. [1981]: Information Aggregation in a Noisy Rational Expectations Economy, Journal of Financial Economics 9, 221-235

Drukarczyk, J. [1980]: Finanzierungstheorie, Verlag Franz Vahlen, München

Dybvig, P.H.; Ingersoll jr., J.E. [1982]: Mean-Variance Theory in Complete Markets, Journal of Business 55, 233-251

Elton, E.J.; Gruber, M.H. [1979]: Portfolio Theory, 25 Years After, North-Holland Publishing Company, Amsterdam-New York-Oxford

Epps, T.W. [1981]: Necessary and Sufficient Conditions for the Mean-Variance Portfolio Model with Constant Risk Aversion, Journal of Financial and Quantitative Analysis 16, 169-176

Faber, M.M. [1970]: Stochastisches Programmieren, Physica-Verlag, Würzburg-Wien

Fama, E.F. [1965]: Portfolio Analysis in a Stable Paretian Market, Management Science 11, 404-419

Fama, E.F. [1970]: Efficient Capital Markets: A Review of Theory and Empirical Work, Journal of Finance 25, 383-417

Fama, E.F.; Laffer, A.B. [1971]: Information and Capital Markets, Journal of Business 44, 289-298

Ferschl, F. [1975]: Nutzen- und Entscheidungstheorie, Westdeutscher Verlag, Opladen

Firchau, V. [1980a]: Wert und maximaler Wert von Informationen für statistische Entscheidungsprobleme, Mathematical Systems in Economics 52, Athenäum, Hain, Scriptor, Hanstein, 1980

Firchau, V. [1980b]: Bounds for the Expected Value of Information, OR-Spektrum 2, 65-73

Firchau, V. [1984]: Der Wert von Renditeprognosen für Anlageentscheidungen, OR-Spektrum 6, 167-176

Franke, G. [1983]: Kapitalmarkt und Separation, Zeitschrift für Betriebswirtschaft 53, 239-260

Goel, P.K. [1983]: Information Measures and Bayesian Hierarchical Models, Journal of the American Statistical Association 78, 408-410

Goel, P.K.; DeGroot, M.H. [1981]: Information about Hyperparameters in Hierarchical Models, Journal of the American Statistical Association 76, 140-147

Goldwerger, J. [1977]: Dynamic Programming for a Stochastic Markovian Process with an Application to the Mean Variance Models, Management Science 23, 612-620

Gonedes, N.J. [1976]: Capital Market Equilibrium for a Class of Heterogeneous Expectations in a Two-Parameter World, Journal of Finance, 31, 1-15

Graybill, F.A. [1969]: Introduction to Matrices with Applications in Statistics, Wadsworth Publishing Company, Inc., Belmont, California

Grettenberg, T.L. [1962]: The Ordering of Finite Experiments, Transactions of the Third Prague Conference on Information Theory, Statistical Decision Functions, Random Processes, 193-206

Grossman, S. [1976]: On the Efficiency of Competitive Stock Markets where Trades have Diverse Information, Journal of Finance 31, 573-585

Grossman, S. [1978]: Further Results on the Informational Efficiency of Competitive Stock Markets, Journal of Economic Theory 18, 81-101

Grossman, S.; Stiglitz, J.E. [1980]: On the Impossibility of Informationally Efficient Markets, The American Economic Review 70, 393-408

Hakansson, N.H.; Kunkel, J.G.; Ohlson, J.A. [1982]: Sufficient and Necessary Conditions for Information to have a Social Value in Pure Exchange, Journal of Finance 37, 1169-1181

Heinkel, R. [1982]: A Theory of Capital Structure Relevance under Imperfect Information, Journal of Finance 37, 1141-1150

Hellwig, M.F. [1980]: On the Aggregation of Information in Competitive Markets, Journal of Economic Theory 22, 477-498

Hilton, R.W. [1981]: The Determinants of Information Value: Synthesizing some General Results, Management Science 27, 57-64

Hirshleifer, J. [1971]: The Private and Social Value of Information and the Reward to Inventive Actitity, The American Economic Review 61, 561-574

Hockmann, H. [1979]: Technische Aktienanalyse und Kapitalmarkteffizienz, Zeitschrift für das gesamte Kreditwesen 8, 335-336

Hsu, D.A. [1982]: A Bayesian Robust Detection of Shift in the Risk Structure of Stock Market Returns, Journal of the American Statistical Association 77, 29-39

Jacob, N.L.; Smith, K.V. [1972]: The Value of Perfect Market Forecasts in Portfolio Selection, Journal of Finance 27, 355-369

Jaffe, J.F. [1975]: On the Use of Public Information in Financial Markets, Journal of Finance 30, 831-839

Jennings, R.H.; Barry, C.B. [1983]: Information Dissemination and Portfolio Choice, Journal of Financial and Quantitative Analysis 18, 1, 1-19

Jennings, R.H.; Starks, L.T.; Fellingham, J.C. [1981]: An Equilibrium Model of Asset Trading with Sequential Information Arrival, Journal of Finance 36, 1, 143-161

Jensen, M.C. [1969]: Risk, the Pricing of Capital Assets, and the Evaluation of Investment Portfolios, Journal of Business 42, 167-247

Jobson, J.D.; Korkie, B. [1980]: Estimation for Markowitz Efficient Portfolios, Journal of the American Statistical Association 75, 544-554

Kalymon, B.A. [1971]: Estimation Risk in the Portfolio Selection Model, Journal of Financial and Quantitative Analysis 6, 559-582

Kanodia, C. [1980]: Effects of Shareholder Information on Corporate Decisions and Capital Market Equilibrium, Econometrica 48, 923-953

Kelly, J.L. [1956]: A New Interpretation of Information Rate, The Bell System Technical Journal 35, July, 917-926

Kim, E.H. [1978]: A Mean-Variance Theory of Optimal Capital Structure and Corporate Debt Capacity, Journal of Finance 33, 45-63

Kofler, E.; Menges, G. [1976]: Entscheidungen bei unvollständiger Information, Springer-Verlag, Berlin-Heidelberg-New York

Kofler, E.; Menges, G.; Fahrion, R.; Huschens, S.; Kuss, U. [1980]: Stochastische partielle Information, Statistische Hefte 2, 160-167

Kunkel, J.G. [1982]: Sufficient Conditions for Public Information to have Social Value in a Production and Exchange Economy, Journal of Finance 37, 1005-1013

Laux, H. [1982]: Entscheidungstheorie, 1. Grundlagen, Springer-Verlag, Berlin-Heidelberg-New York

LaValle, I.H. [1968]: On Cash Equivalents and Information Evaluation in Decisions under Uncertainty, Part I,II,III, American Statistical Association Journal 63, 252-290

LaValle, I.H. [1970]: An Introduction to Probability, Decision and Inference, International Series in Decision Processes, New York

Levy, H.; Kroll, Y. [1980]: Sample vs. Population Mean-Variance Efficient Portfolios, Management Science 26, 11, 1108-1116

Levy, H.; Markowitz, H.M. [1979]: Approximating Expected Utility by a Function of Mean and Variance, American Economic Review 69, 308-317

Lin, W.T. [1981]: A Minimum Bayes Risk Approach to Optimal Portfolio Choice, International Journal of Systems Science 12, 495-509

Lin, W.T.; Boot, J.C.G. [1982]: A Linear Decision Analysis Model of Optimal Portfolio Investments, International Journal of Systems Sciences 13, 469-489

Lindley, D.V. [1955]: On a Measure of the Information Provided by an Experiment, Ann. Math. Stat. 27, 986-1005

Lintner, J. [1965]: Security Prices, Risk, and Maximal Gains from Diversification, Journal of Finance 20, 587-615

Lintner, J. [1969]: The Aggregation of Investor's Diverse Judgements and Preferences in Purely Competitive Security Markets, Journal of Financial and Quantitative Analysis 4, 347-400

Mag, W. [1977]: Entscheidung und Information, Verlag Franz Vahlen, München

Maier, S.F.; Peterson, D.W.; Van der Weide, J.H. [1982]: An Empirical Bayes Estimate of Market Risk, Management Science 28, 728-737

Mao, J.C.T.; Särndal, C.E. [1966]: A Decision Theory Approach to Portfolio Selection, Management Science 12, B323-B333

Marschak, J. [1954]: Towards an Economic Theory of Organisation and Information, Decision Processes (Coombs, Thrall, Davis), New York, 187-220

Marschak, J. [1959]: Remarks on the Economics of Information, Contributions to Scientific Research in Management, 79-98

Marschak, J. [1971]: Economics of Information Systems, Journal of the American Statistical Association 66, 333, 192-219

Markowitz, H. [1952]: Portfolio Selection, Journal of Finance, 77-91

Merton, R.C. [1972]: An Analytic Derivation of the Efficient Portfolio Frontier, Journal of Financial and Quantitative Analysis, 1851-1872

Merton, R.C. [1981]: On Market Timing and Investment Performance, Journal of Business 54, 363-406

Modigliani, F.; Miller, M.H. [1958]: The Cost of Capital, Corporation Finance and the Theory of Investment, American Economic Review 48, 261-267

Möller, H.P. [1983]: Probleme und Ergebnisse kaptialmarktorientierter empirischer Bilanzforschung in Deutschland, Betriebswirtschaftliche Forschung und Praxis 35, 285-302

Morris, J.R. [1974]: The Logarithmic Investor's Decision to Aquire Costly Information, Management Science 21, 383-391

Mossin, J. [1966]: Equilibrium in a Capital Asset Market, Econometrica 34, 141-183

Mossin, J. [1968]: Optimal Multiperiod Portfolio Policies, Journal of Business 41, 215-229

Mossin, J. [1973]: Theory of Financial Markets, Prentice-Hall, Inc., Englewood Cliffs, New York

Nachman, D.C. [1975]: Risk Aversion, Impatience, and Optimal Timing Decisions, Journal of Economic Theory 11, 196-246

Niggemann, W. [1973]: Optimale Informationsprozesse in betriebswirtschaftlichen Entscheidungssituationen, Betriebswirtschaftlicher Verlag Dr. Th. Gabler, Wiesbaden

Norgaard, R.; Killeen, T. [1980]: Expected Utility and the Truncated Normal Distribution, Management Science 26, 901-909

Ohlson, J.A. [1975]: The Complete Ordering of Information Alternatives for a Class of Portfolio Selection Models, Journal of Accounting Research 13, 267-282

Owen, J.; Rabinovitch, R. [1980]: The Cost of Information and Equilibrium in the Capital Asset Market, Journal of Financial and Quantitative Analysis 15, 497-508

Owen, J.; Rabinovitch, R. [1983]: On the Class of Elliptical Distributions and their Applications to the Theory of Portfolio Choice, Journal of Finance 38, 745-752

Patel, N.R.; Subrahmanyam, M.G. [1982]: A Simple Algorithm for Optimal Portfolio Selection with Fixed Transaction Costs, Management Science 28, 303-314

Perry, P.R. [1983]: More Evidence on the Nature of the Distribution of Security Returns, Journal of Financial and Quanitative Analysis 18, 211-221

Peterson, D.; Peterson, P. [1982]: The Effect of Changing Expectations upon Stock Returns, Journal of Financial and Quantitative Analysis 17, 799-813

Pfanzagl, J. [1959]: Die axiomatischen Grundlagen einer allgemeinen Theorie des Messens, Würzburg

Philippatos, G.C.; Gressis, N. [1975]: Conditions of Equivalence among E-V, SSD, and E-H Portfolio Selection Criteria: The Case for Uniform, Normal, and Lognormal Distributions, Management Science 21, 617-625

Pratt, J.W. [1964]: Risk Aversion in the Small and in the Large, Econometrica 32, 122-136

Pratt, J.W.; Raiffa, H.; Schlaifer, R. [1965]: Introduction to Statistical Decision Theory, McGraw-Hill, New York

Pulley, L.B. [1983]: Mean-Variance Approximations to Expected Logarithmic Utility, Operations Research 31, 685-696

Rabinovitch, R.; Owen, J. [1978]: Nonhomogenous Expectations and Information in the Capital Asset Market, Journal of Finance 33, 575-587

Raiffa, H.; Schlaifer, R. [1961]: Applied Statistical Decision Theory, Boston

Rehberg, J. [1973]: Wert und Kosten von Informationen, Verlag Harri Deutsch, Frankfurt/Main-Zürich

Rembold, J.Th. [1977]: Stochastische lineare Optimierung, Verlag Anton Hain, Meisenheim

Richter, H. [1963]: Subjektive Wahrscheinlichkeit und multisubjektive Tests, Zeitschrift für Wahrscheinlichkeitstheorie 1, 271-277

Rockafellar, R.T. [1970]: Convex Analysis, Princeton, University Press

Roll, R. [1977]: A Critique of the Asset Pricing Theory's Tests, Journal of Financial Economics 4, 129-176

Ross, S.A. [1978]: Mutual Fund Separation in Financial Theory - The Separating Distributions, Journal of Economic Theory 17, 254-286

Rothschild, M.; Stiglitz, J.E. [1970]: Increasing Risk: I. A Definition, Journal of Economic Theory 2, 225-243

Rudolph, B. [1979]: Kapitalkosten bei unsicheren Erwartungen, Springer-Verlag, Berlin-Heidelberg-New York

Rudolph, B. [1982]: Portefeuille- und Aktienkursbildung bei monopolistischem Anlegerwettbewerb, Zeitschrift für Betriebswirtschaft 52, 471-490

Rudolph, B. [1983]: Zur Bedeutung der kapitaltheoretischen Separationstheoreme für die Investitionsplanung, Zeitschrift für Betriebswirtschaft 53, 261-287

Saelzle, R. [1976]: Investitionsentscheidungen und Kapitalmarkttheorie, Betriebswirtschaftlicher Verlag, Dr. Th. Gabler, Wiesbaden

Schnabel, J.A. [1981]: Dividend Policy, Liquidity Needs, and the Equilibrium Valuation of Shares, International Journal of Systems Sciences 12, 1365-1378

Schneeweiß, H. [1967]: Entscheidungskriterien bei Risiko, Springer-Verlag, Berlin-Heidelberg-New York

Shannon, C.E. [1948]: The Mathematical Theory of Communication, Bell Systems Technical Journal 27

Shannon, C.E.; Weaver, W. [1949]: The Mathematical Theory of Communication, The University of Illinois Press

Sharpe, W. [1964]: Capital Asset Prices: A Theory of Market Equilibrium under Conditions of Risk, Journal of Finance 19, 425-442

Sharpe, W. [1970]: Portfolio Theory and Capital Markets, McGraw-Hill Book Company, New York

Sinn, H.-W. [1980]: Ökonomische Entscheidungen bei Ungewißheit, Mohr-Verlag, Tübingen

Smith, S.A. [1974]: A Derivation of Entropy and the Maximum Entropy Criterion in the Context of Decision Problems, IEEE Transactions on Systems, Man, and Cybernetics, 4, 2, 157-163

Spremann, K.; Bamberg, G. [1980]: Modigliani-Miller Thesen, Konkursrisiko und Bilanzpolitik, Arbeitspapiere zur Mathematischen Wirtschaftsforschung, Heft 43, Augsburg

Spremann, K.; Bamberg, G. [1981]: Bilanzpolitik, Mehrperioden-Diversifikation und kapitaltheoretische Unternehmenswerte, Zeitschrift für Betriebswirtschaft 51, 1204-1222

Spremann, K.; Bamberg, G. [1983a]: Emissionslimitierung und Kursbildung in einem unvollkommenen Kapitalmarkt, Zeitschrift für betriebswirtschaftliche Forschung 35, 302-314

Spremann, K.; Bamberg, G. [1983b]: Local Consistency of Risk Preferences, Statistische Hefte 24, 73-83

Swoboda, P. [1981]: Betriebliche Finanzierung, Physica-Verlag, Würzburg-Wien

Swoboda, P. [1982]: Heterogene Information und Kapitalstruktur der Unternehmung, Zeitschrift für betriebswirtschaftliche Forschung 34, 705-727

Teichmann, H. [1973]: Zum Wert und Preis von Informationen, Zeitschrift für Betriebswirtschaft, 373-390

Tobin, J. [1968]: Liquidity Preference as Behavior Toward Risk, The Review of Economic Studies 25, 65-86

Tobin, J. [1983]: Liquidity Preference, Separation, and Asset Pricing, Zeitschrift für Betriebswirtschaft 53, 236-238

Wahl, J. [1983]: Informationsbewertung und -effizeinz auf dem Kapitalmarkt, Physica-Verlag, Würzburg-Wien

Watts, R. [1973]: The Information Content of Dividends, Journal of Business 46, 191-211

Wenzel, F. [1975]: Entscheidungsorientierte Informationsbewertung, Opladen

Wild, J. [1971]: Zur Problematik der Nutzenbewertung von Informationen, Zeitschrift für Betriebswirtschaft, 315-334

Wilhelm, J. [1981]: Zum Verhältnis von Capital Asset Pricing Model, Arbitrage Pricing Theory und Bedingungen der Arbitragefreiheit von Finanzmärkten, Zeitschrift für betriebswirtschaftliche Forschung 33, 891-905

Wilhelm, J. [1983]: Finanztitelmärkte und Unternehmensfinanzierung, Springer-Verlag, Berlin-Heidelberg-New York

Wilhelm, J. [1985]: Arbitrage Theory, Springer-Verlag, Berlin-Heidelberg-New York

Winkler, R.L.; Barry, C.B. [1975]: A Bayesian Model for Portfolio Selection and Revision, Journal of Finance 30, 179-192

Wittmann, W. [1959]: Unternehmung und unvollkommene Information, Köln-Opladen.

Vol. 184: R. E. Burkard and U. Derigs, Assignment and Matching Problems: Solution Methods with FORTRAN-Programs. VIII, 148 pages. 1980.

Vol. 185: C. C. von Weizsäcker, Barriers to Entry. VI, 220 pages. 1980.

Vol. 186: Ch.-L. Hwang and K. Yoon, Multiple Attribute Decision Making – Methods and Applications. A State-of-the-Art-Survey. XI, 259 pages. 1981.

Vol. 187: W. Hock, K. Schittkowski, Test Examples for Nonlinear Programming Codes. V. 178 pages. 1981.

Vol. 188: D. Bös, Economic Theory of Public Enterprise. VII, 142 pages. 1981.

Vol. 189: A. P. Lüthi, Messung wirtschaftlicher Ungleichheit. IX, 287 pages. 1981.

Vol. 190: J. N. Morse, Organizations: Multiple Agents with Multiple Criteria. Proceedings, 1980. VI, 509 pages. 1981.

Vol. 191: H. R. Sneessens, Theory and Estimation of Macroeconomic Rationing Models. VII, 138 pages. 1981.

Vol. 192: H. J. Bierens: Robust Methods and Asymptotic Theory in Nonlinear Econometrics. IX, 198 pages. 1981.

Vol. 193: J. K. Sengupta, Optimal Decisions under Uncertainty. VII, 156 pages. 1981.

Vol. 194: R. W. Shephard, Cost and Production Functions. XI, 104 pages. 1981.

Vol. 195: H. W. Ursprung, Die elementare Katastrophentheorie. Eine Darstellung aus der Sicht der Ökonomie. VII, 332 pages. 1982.

Vol. 196: M. Nermuth, Information Structures in Economics. VIII, 236 pages. 1982.

Vol. 197: Integer Programming and Related Areas. A Classified Bibliography. 1978 – 1981. Edited by R. von Randow. XIV, 338 pages. 1982.

Vol. 198: P. Zweifel, Ein ökonomisches Modell des Arztverhaltens. XIX, 392 Seiten. 1982.

Vol. 199: Evaluating Mathematical Programming Techniques. Proceedings, 1981. Edited by J.M. Mulvey. XI, 379 pages. 1982.

Vol. 200: The Resource Sector in an Open Economy. Edited by H. Siebert. IX, 161 pages. 1984.

Vol. 201: P. M. C. de Boer, Price Effects in Input-Output-Relations: A Theoretical and Empirical Study for the Netherlands 1949–1967. X, 140 pages. 1982.

Vol. 202: U. Witt, J. Perske, SMS – A Program Package for Simulation and Gaming of Stochastic Market Processes and Learning Behavior. VII, 266 pages. 1982.

Vol. 203: Compilation of Input-Output Tables. Proceedings, 1981. Edited by J. V. Skolka. VII, 307 pages. 1982.

Vol. 204: K. C. Mosler, Entscheidungsregeln bei Risiko: Multivariate stochastische Dominanz. VII, 172 Seiten. 1982.

Vol. 205: R. Ramanathan, Introduction to the Theory of Economic Growth. IX, 347 pages. 1982.

Vol. 206: M. H. Karwan, V. Lotfi, J. Telgen, and S. Zionts, Redundancy in Mathematical Programming. VII, 286 pages. 1983.

Vol. 207: Y. Fujimori, Modern Analysis of Value Theory. X, 165 pages. 1982.

Vol. 208: Econometric Decision Models. Proceedings, 1981. Edited by J. Gruber. VI, 364 pages. 1983.

Vol. 209: Essays and Surveys on Multiple Criteria Decision Making. Proceedings, 1982. Edited by P. Hansen. VII, 441 pages. 1983.

Vol. 210: Technology, Organization and Economic Structure. Edited by R. Sato and M. J. Beckmann. VIII, 195 pages. 1983.

Vol. 211: P. van den Heuvel, The Stability of a Macroeconomic System with Quantity Constraints. VII, 169 pages. 1983.

Vol. 212: R. Sato and T. Nôno, Invariance Principles and the Structure of Technology. V, 94 pages. 1983.

Vol. 213: Aspiration Levels in Bargaining and Economic Decision Making. Proceedings, 1982. Edited by R. Tietz. VIII, 406 pages. 1983.

Vol. 214: M. Faber, H. Niemes und G. Stephan, Entropie, Umweltschutz und Rohstoffverbrauch. IX, 181 Seiten. 1983.

Vol. 215: Semi-Infinite Programming and Applications. Proceedings, 1981. Edited by A. V. Fiacco and K. O. Kortanek. XI, 322 pages. 1983.

Vol. 216: H. H. Müller, Fiscal Policies in a General Equilibrium Model with Persistent Unemployment. VI, 92 pages. 1983.

Vol. 217: Ch. Grootaert, The Relation Between Final Demand and Income Distribution. XIV, 105 pages. 1983.

Vol. 218: P. van Loon, A Dynamic Theory of the Firm: Production, Finance and Investment. VII, 191 pages. 1983.

Vol. 219: E. van Damme, Refinements of the Nash Equilibrium Concept. VI, 151 pages. 1983.

Vol. 220: M. Aoki, Notes on Economic Time Series Analysis: System Theoretic Perspectives. IX, 249 pages. 1983.

Vol. 221: S. Nakamura, An Inter-Industry Translog Model of Prices and Technical Change for the West German Economy. XIV, 290 pages. 1984.

Vol. 222: P. Meier, Energy Systems Analysis for Developing Countries. VI, 344 pages. 1984.

Vol. 223: W. Trockel, Market Demand. VIII, 205 pages. 1984.

Vol. 224: M. Kiy, Ein disaggregiertes Prognosesystem für die Bundesrepublik Deutschland. XVIII, 276 Seiten. 1984.

Vol. 225: T. R. von Ungern-Sternberg, Zur Analyse von Märkten mit unvollständiger Nachfragerinformation. IX, 125 Seiten. 1984

Vol. 226: Selected Topics in Operations Research and Mathematical Economics. Proceedings, 1983. Edited by G. Hammer and D. Pallaschke. IX, 478 pages. 1984.

Vol. 227: Risk and Capital. Proceedings, 1983. Edited by G. Bamberg and K. Spremann. VII, 306 pages. 1984.

Vol. 228: Nonlinear Models of Fluctuating Growth. Proceedings, 1983. Edited by R. M. Goodwin, M. Krüger and A. Vercelli. XVII, 277 pages. 1984.

Vol. 229: Interactive Decision Analysis. Proceedings, 1983. Edited by M. Grauer and A. P. Wierzbicki. VIII, 269 pages. 1984.

Vol. 230: Macro-Economic Planning with Conflicting Goals. Proceedings, 1982. Edited by M. Despontin, P. Nijkamp and J. Spronk. VI, 297 pages. 1984.

Vol. 231: G. F. Newell, The M/M/∞ Service System with Ranked Servers in Heavy Traffic. XI, 126 pages. 1984.

Vol. 232: L. Bauwens, Bayesian Full Information Analysis of Simultaneous Equation Models Using Integration by Monte Carlo. VI, 114 pages. 1984.

Vol. 233: G. Wagenhals, The World Copper Market. XI, 190 pages. 1984.

Vol. 234: B.C. Eaves, A Course in Triangulations for Solving Equations with Deformations. III, 302 pages. 1984.

Vol. 235: Stochastic Models in Reliability Theory. Proceedings, 1984. Edited by S. Osaki and Y. Hatoyama. VII, 212 pages. 1984.

Vol. 236: G. Gandolfo, P.C. Padoan, A Disequilibrium Model of Real and Financial Accumulation in an Open Economy. VI, 172 pages. 1984.

Vol. 237: Misspecification Analysis. Proceedings, 1983. Edited by T. K. Dijkstra. V, 129 pages. 1984.

Vol. 238: W. Domschke, A. Drexl, Location and Layout Planning. IV, 134 pages. 1985.

Vol. 239: Microeconomic Models of Housing Markets. Edited by K. Stahl. VII, 197 pages. 1985.

Vol. 240: Contributions to Operations Research. Proceedings, 1984. Edited by K. Neumann and D. Pallaschke. V, 190 pages. 1985.

Vol. 241: U. Wittmann, Das Konzept rationaler Preiserwartungen. XI, 310 Seiten. 1985.

Vol. 242: Decision Making with Multiple Objectives. Proceedings, 1984. Edited by Y.Y. Haimes and V. Chankong. XI, 571 pages. 1985.

Vol. 243: Integer Programming and Related Areas. A Classified Bibliography 1981–1984. Edited by R. von Randow. XX, 386 pages. 1985.

Vol. 244: Advances in Equilibrium Theory. Proceedings, 1984. Edited by C.D. Aliprantis, O. Burkinshaw and N.J. Rothman. II, 235 pages. 1985.

Vol. 245: J.E.M. Wilhelm, Arbitrage Theory. VII, 114 pages. 1985.

Vol. 246: P.W. Otter, Dynamic Feature Space Modelling, Filtering and Self-Tuning Control of Stochastic Systems. XIV, 177 pages. 1985.

Vol. 247: Optimization and Discrete Ch
Proceedings, 1983. Edited by B.G. Hutc
M. Batty. VI, 371 pages. 1985.

Vol. 248: Plural Rationality and Interactive Decision Processes. Proceedings, 1984. Edited by M. Grauer, M. Thompson and A.P. Wierzbicki. VI, 354 pages. 1985.

Vol. 249: Spatial Price Equilibrium: Advances in Theory, Computation and Application. Proceedings, 1984. Edited by P. T. Harker. VII, 277 pages. 1985.

Vol. 250: M. Roubens, Ph. Vincke, Preference Modelling. VIII, 94 pages. 1985.

Vol. 251: Input-Output Modeling. Proceedings, 1984. Edited by A. Smyshlyaev. VI, 261 pages. 1985.

Vol. 252: A. Birolini, On the Use of Stochastic Processes in Modeling Reliability Problems. VI, 105 pages. 1985.

Vol. 253: C. Withagen, Economic Theory and International Trade in Natural Exhaustible Resources. VI, 172 pages. 1985.

Vol. 254: S. Müller, Arbitrage Pricing of Contingent Claims. VIII, 151 pages. 1985.

Vol. 255: Nondifferentiable Optimization: Motivations and Applications. Proceedings, 1984. Edited by V.F. Demyanov and D. Pallaschke. VI, 350 pages. 1985.

Vol. 256: Convexity and Duality in Optimization. Proceedings, 1984. Edited by J. Ponstein. V, 142 pages. 1985.

Vol. 257: Dynamics of Macrosystems. Proceedings, 1984. Edited by J.-P. Aubin, D. Saari and K. Sigmund. VI, 280 pages. 1985.

Vol. 258: H. Funke, Eine allgemeine Theorie der Polypol- und Oligopolpreisbildung. III, 237 pages. 1985.

Vol. 259: Infinite Programming. Proceedings, 1984. Edited by E.J. Anderson and A.B. Philpott. XIV, 244 pages. 1985.

Vol. 260: H.-J. Kruse, Degeneracy Graphs and the Neighbourhood Problem. VIII, 128 pages. 1986.

Vol. 261: Th.R. Gulledge, Jr., N.K. Womer, The Economics of Made-to-Order Production. VI, 134 pages. 1986.

Vol. 262: H.U. Buhl, A Neo-Classical Theory of Distribution and Wealth. V, 146 pages. 1986.

Vol. 263: M. Schäfer, Resource Extraction and Market Structure. XI, 154 pages. 1986.

Vol. 264: Models of Economic Dynamics. Proceedings, 1983. Edited by H.F. Sonnenschein. VII, 212 pages. 1986.

Vol. 265: Dynamic Games and Applications in Economics. Edited by T. Başar. IX, 288 pages. 1986.

Vol. 266: Multi-Stage Production Planning and Inventory Control. Edited by S. Axsäter, Ch. Schneeweiss and E. Silver. V, 264 pages. 1986.

Vol. 267: R. Bemelmans, The Capacity Aspect of Inventories. IX, 165 pages. 1986.

Vol. 268: V. Firchau, Information Evaluation in Capital Markets. VII, 103 pages. 1986.

GPSR Compliance

The European Union's (EU) General Product Safety Regulation (GPSR) is a set of rules that requires consumer products to be safe and our obligations to ensure this.

If you have any concerns about our products, you can contact us on ProductSafety@springernature.com

In case Publisher is established outside the EU, the EU authorized representative is:

Springer Nature Customer Service Center GmbH
Europaplatz 3
69115 Heidelberg, Germany

Batch number: 10844827

Printed by Printforce, the Netherlands